Praise for The Cello Who Loved Me:

"After hearing a virtuoso during a pilgrimage in Spain, Sorensen was hooked on learning the cello, an instrument he'd never touched before. What follows is a journey toward enlightenment that led from a surprisingly expert teacher in the music store adjoining a Costa Rican restaurant down the street, to various luthiers, cellists, and other professionals, and an ultimate and lofty goal of playing 'Here Comes the Sun' on a Stradivarius. Whether it was too lofty didn't matter, because along the way he discovered that 'playing became more like spending time with an old friend, rather than being trapped in a bad conversation I wanted to escape,' and a new way of seeing life.

"Told with equal parts of exuberance, reflection, and humor, Sorensen takes us along with him on his pilgrimage to learn the cello and explore his musical roots. More than this, his is a story of inspiration we could all use to pursue our own passions."

Jason Kilgore—author of *Dragon of the Federation* and creator of the Strange Worlds of Jason Kilgore

"From the sunny slopes of the Camino de Santiago, to the dark recesses under the dashboard of a '64 Volvo, and on to finding his Holy Grail in the catacombs of the National Museum of American History, Sorensen takes the reader on a personal quest to uncover the heart and soul of a musical instrument: the cello. He tells his story with humor, insight, and an eye for detail, and the various 'side quests'—ranging from battles with an evil high school music teacher to eating moose stew in Norway—are as much fun to read about as his journey to mastering this challenging and inspiring musical instrument."

William Erickson—Beaverton, Oregon

"George's new book is the phantasmagoria of a fantastic sequence of ever-changing opportunities and dreams come true. He began playing the cello, while others his age were napping quietly in a comfortable chair."

Mary Ann Coggins Kaza—music teacher, professional violinist for 50+ years

"This book hooked me from the start. The author shared his experience on the Camino de Santiago and his final days on the trail, where his passion was ignited. A final dinner followed by a lecture and a performance by a professional cellist. During that professional performance by this cello master, the author found love in the cello's voice.

"The voice of the cello spoke to the author, and he set about on another pilgrimage, a quest for knowledge and acquiring the skill of the strings. From then on, the author leads the reader on his journey in the discovery of his passion. He shows the roots of his joy in the beautiful construction, the components of the instrument, and the history of its development.

"This is a wonderful read for any student of the cello. It is full of history, humor, and the intricacies of the cello. I recommend it heartily."

David Normand—essayist, poet, blogger

"What stood out to me when George visited my workshop was how deeply he wanted to understand the cello. He wasn't just curious about how it's made, but about why it moves people. Spending time with him made me see the cello's beauty with fresh eyes."

Michael Doran—award winning cello luthier, Duvall, Washington

"Blending high and low notes from his life, George presents his harmonious story as 'a seasoned, but nonetheless spunky, adult beginner' starting cello lessons at 71. His musical journey proves that there's no age limit on learning. And that having bad teachers in the past shouldn't prevent you from pursuing your passion now."

— J. Nollet

THE CELLO WHO LOVED ME

An accidental pilgrimage to master the world's most beautiful instrument

George Sorensen

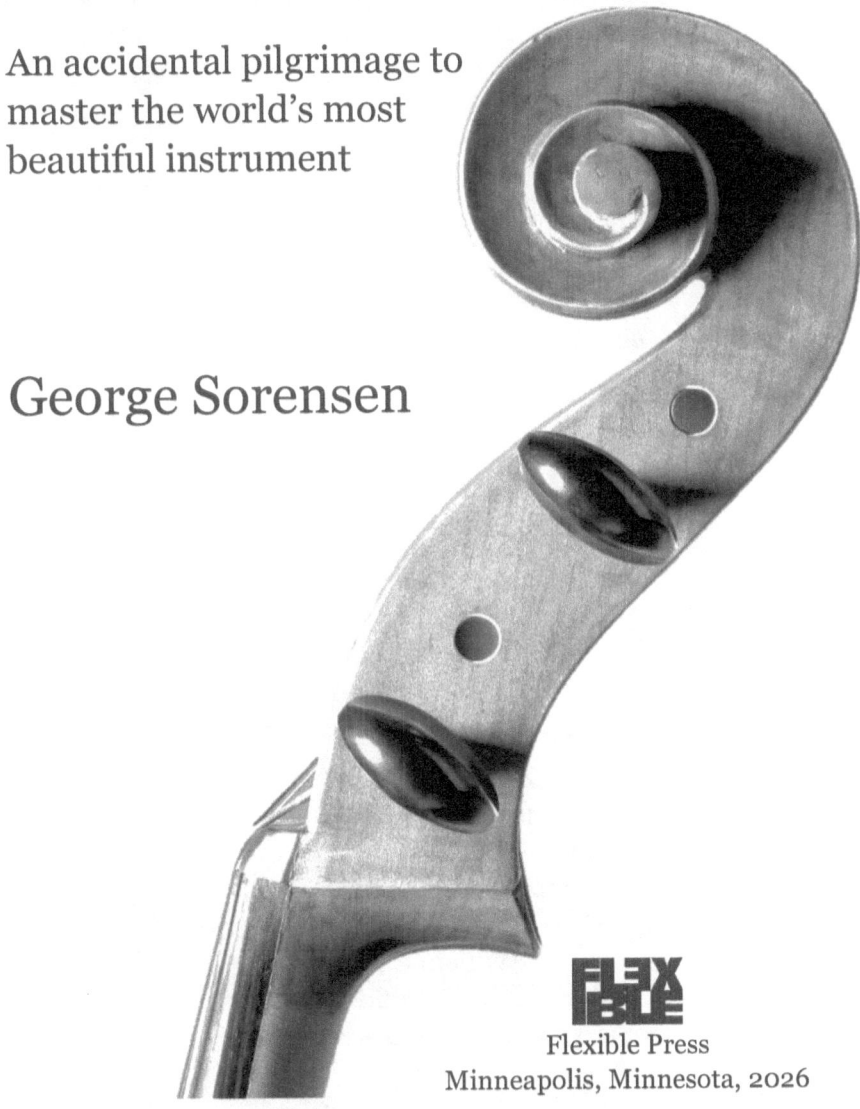

FL=X
IBLE
Flexible Press
Minneapolis, Minnesota, 2026

Print ISBN: 979-8-9998771-1-6
eBook ISBN: 979-8-9998771-2-3

Flexible Press LLC
Minneapolis, Minnesota
www.flexiblepub.com
Editors William E Burleson
Vicki Adang, Mark My Words Editorial Services, LLC
Cover: William E Burleson
Author photos: Bradley Sellers
Cello photo: DNY59, Getty Images Signature, via Canva

For my amazing daughter
Kenzy Blythe Redhawk Sorensen
and the Will C. Crawford High School Class of 1969
San Diego, California

The Cello Who Loved Me

By George Sorensen

Chapter 1
The Unlikely Pilgrim

When I turned seventy-one, I decided to play the cello while walking the Camino de Santiago across the north of Spain.

Committing to follow the Camino makes you a pilgrim, and that's how people refer to you when you are there. Whether aware of it or not, those who make this pilgrimage are in the midst of a spiritual journey—large or small. I certainly didn't think of this adventure as anything more than completing a celebrated hike—at first. Expecting nothing unusual to happen is evidently key to the pilgrim experience, as I had no expectations about anything out of the ordinary occurring.

We followed the ancient route known as the Camino Francés, as the official starting point is located across the border in Saint Jean, France. Many routes can be followed, but all weave their way to the Cathedral of Santiago de Compostela. The remains of Saint James the Apostle are believed to be enshrined in a reliquary there, and pilgrims have made the cathedral a sacred destination for more than a thousand years.

Our group picked up the trail in Pamplona, the town made famous by Hemingway and the running of the bulls. From there, we skipped along the trail, or more specifically, took a smooth-riding tour bus to our trailhead each day so we could walk another section. It was, after all, an accommodating National Geographic Expedition.

As we walked, we learned why Spain has such a charming reputation. We encountered sedate churches and overwhelming cathedrals. Even in the smallest of villages there are sacred places with their own peculiarities and stories.

Each evening we stayed in a contemporary hotel or, better yet, a *parador*—a centuries-old monastery or convent made of great granite blocks with timeless archways and stone floors. I could imagine monks contemplating their state of being or singing harmonic carols down the cavernous stairways to what are now full bars and Michelin-star quality restaurants. The Spanish government renovated these once-abandoned buildings into upscale hotels. Most are in the middle of a village or city and near a historic church.

I do not remember much talk about this being a pilgrim's journey or how fellow hikers were processing their saintly experiences, assuming they were having any. If a fellow traveler had a transcendent ambition of any kind or thought of being a pilgrim as a transformative event, I never heard about their goals.

That said, there were plenty of stories in the news about folks searching for spiritual roots. Loneliness and a lack of community drain people of their love of living. Plenty of us recognized our lives are missing something, without knowing what that might be. On top of everything else, we were well into the twenty-first century, which had started rough with the shock of terrorism and grew worse with the rise of petty dictators heaving hatred in all directions.

I figured the Camino would offer a hot, dry, picturesque journey. I was just going for a tramp on a famous path, as I've been an avid hiker since my Cub Scout pack went camping and my days in a Boy Scout troop.

On the other hand, self-exploration experiences like this have, for centuries, opened up the souls of those who follow the route so they might make discoveries about themselves. The most unsuspecting of us are visited by angels who are disguised or so goes the oft quoted verse, "Be not forgetful to entertain strangers: for thereby some have entertained angels unawares."

I like the sense that there is potential to be inspired by an encounter with just about anybody, including an angel, without my knowledge. A pilgrimage on the Camino provides a place for this to happen, by combining physical exertion with plenty of time to think as you take step after step with people you just met in a stimulating, sometimes sacred environment.

Oddly enough, a life-changing experience happened to me, just not in the way I might have imagined. A lightning bolt of revelation didn't knock me to the ground. I simply realized I'd been attracted to something for a long time without being aware. Perhaps it was to fill a void I did not know I had.

During the several days we'd been hiking, our guides hinted at a special event coming up toward the end of our journey. "It's a surprise. I don't want to tell you anything about it," our guide Maria said. "You will enjoy what we have for you. You will see when we get there."

Parador de Villafranca del Bierzo

Our hotel this night sat up in the airy hills of Galicia in the northwest corner of Spain where there was a tranquility you don't find in the popular tourist areas. Instead of a converted monastery, this place sported a lot of large glass windows, wooden floors rather than stone, even views of pine trees from the upstairs rooms. After days of following the Camino through sunflower fields with little shade in September weather, we'd arrived in a setting with the cool alpine feel of forested slopes.

Once checked in, showered, and changed, our fellow hikers met in the contemporary lobby for this long-promised presentation. All the itinerary indicated was that we'd "meet with a local historian before dinner."

After the usual Spanish casualness about schedules, we were ushered into an angular room with more glass walls. A low stage large enough for a jazz trio rose from the near end of the room.

A tall man with a mass of tangled, curly black hair tumbling to his shoulders greeted us as we entered. His look suggested he could have been both an earthy bohemian artist and the swarthy captain of a Spanish galleon in a previous life. I felt his presence filling the room.

"Hello, welcome," he said with the resonance of someone who spends a great deal of time onstage in front of an audience. "I am Carlos Ariel Gracia Báez—musician, conductor, teacher."

Carlos went on to congratulate us on undertaking the Camino and explained how he intended to provide an enriching hour before dinner—a presentation of music and culture. "I brought with me an interesting friend." He stepped to the back of the compact stage where he picked up his russet-hued instrument the size of a child.

He held the instrument aloft by the neck. "Do you know what this is?"

"A cello," we replied as a chorus.

"Do you know the cello?" Carlos asked as he adjusted a single chair at the stage apron. No one admitted to knowing anything about the instrument.

I'd always enjoyed listening to the cello. The tone is rich and warm. Watching a cellist who has mastered the instrument is pleasurable—plus playing the cello looks remarkably relaxed compared to, say, playing a violin. A violinist's left arm is scrunched up and their hand turned uncomfortably around.

I'd seen the cello played in person occasionally. In high school, I blew on the trombone while sitting behind the string section in the orchestra two or three times a year. The cello can hit some lower notes the way bass instruments such as the tuba or bass guitar can, while they play a moving bass line for the rest of the music ride on. The cello also reaches up to touch the register where the violin plays.

For an hour, Carlos dialogued with our group of pilgrims, discussing a classical music theme or talking about a musical experience. Then he introduced what he would play, then stood, bowed formally to the audience, sat back down in his chair, and arranged himself into position with the cello. Listening to him play was like sitting before a warm, cozy fire. With accuracy and emotion, Carlos went on to perform a classical repertoire.

My wife, Susan, and I sat in the seats nearest the stage to hear with great clarity the affable sounds. We watched him rock with the instrument, as cellists do. He steadied the cello with his knees, a bow in one hand, as the other hand picked out the notes on the fingerboard. The performance turned my thoughts from the weariness of the world toward a less-troubled place.

At the conclusion of each classical selection, he stood and bowed again.

"Bach is the greatest composer of all time, without a doubt. I love Bach," Carlos stated. "What would you like me to play?"

A man asked for the second movement of some symphony nobody'd ever heard of. Carlos smiled but could not dig up anything on this.

I said, "*The Brandenburg Concertos*?"

Carlos looked at me with dazed bemusement. "That is not possible. One of them needs a small trumpet. Did you bring one?" he said, drawing laughs.

"You said you like Bach," I explained.

"They are beautiful but need many more musicians. The *Brandenburgs* are much too much for one musician, but here's what I will do. I will play the themes from each."

At that, he bent at the waist once more, plunked down in his chair, and played the musical theme from each of the concertos without having to think through which went where. One after the other, preceded by a brief introduction, Carlos performed the distinctive leitmotif for each. He sounded fully rehearsed, lively, as if he'd planned the arrangement in advance.

The hour went quickly, with Carlos in conversation with us about culture and music, wrapping these into his beloved Bach and telling stories about the Spanish soul, conducting, and the greater world of the musical arts.

Toward the end, another person from our group asked, "Can you play 'God Save the King'?"

A poignant request, as Queen Elizabeth II had passed away just the week before. Susan and I had been in London, working our way to the start of the Camino. We were ordering dinner at a restaurant when the news hit. The next day, we were scheduled to tour Buckingham Palace. With the tour canceled, we went to the palace early in the morning to be among the first to share our sympathy at the palace gates. The energy from that emotional experience was still with us many days later at this cello concert. A feeling of unity and loss.

"Of course," Carlos said without hesitation, launching to a buoyant rendition of the tune, which sounded both respectful and hopeful.

Although I am unable to put my finger on any particular moment, at some point in the evening, I became enchanted by the instrument this ardent Spaniard played with so much ease and enthusiasm. I wanted to feel as effortless creating elegant music as Carlos was. I wished to become the man playing the cello.

Chapter 2
Lessons

We returned to our home near Portland. Not the Portland with all the lobsters, rather the one in Oregon that used to be a lumber town and is now all about running shoes. I'd shared my enjoyment of the cello performance we'd attended during our Camino with Susan, but not my interest in learning to play and what might be involved. This was because I didn't have a plan yet to pursue it, didn't know any cello players, or how to begin the journey. So long as it wasn't a major expense and didn't interfere with anything else we were doing, I thought I'd hold off filling her in until I came up with a plan.

We'd been together over thirty years and had two grown children, so I pretty much knew what I could get away with at this point.

I scoured the city for the right cello teacher.

The problem, I picked up on right away, was there wasn't a smorgasbord of teachers from which to choose. Portland is a village with a lot of people—not a big city, despite its size. The metropolitan area population is pushing three million, so traffic can be bad in places, and the homelessness, vandalism, and other problems are similar to those of other communities this size. However, there isn't a sense you're in an electrifying economic hub or that something important will happen here.

Oregonians look two hundred miles north to Seattle for a global center with whatever big-city enchantments they might desire: a big harbor, the Space Needle, seaside Ferris wheel, an economic tidal wave of company operations such as Amazon, Microsoft, Nordstrom, Tommy Bahama, Starbucks, REI, and Boeing.

My sense of being stuck with a limited pool of options left me wondering: How many people who play the cello could there be in

Portland? How many cello teachers dwell among us? Not all accomplished cellists want to give lessons. Of those who are good at teaching, would any of them have an opening in their schedule and be able to deal with the idiosyncrasies of a seasoned, but nonetheless spunky, adult beginner—the polite category I fell into?

One small music store and school was conveniently close. However, Lake Music hadn't struck me as the right place because of its focus on lessons for school-age kids.

I remember the shop from the brief time my daughter and son took lessons there, for it being stacked with used instruments for rent. The place hadn't been updated since Elvis sang "Blue Suede Shoes." Really, it felt like the 1950s inside the shop, though it first opened its doors in 1970.

Even if Lake Music had a cello teacher, I suspected they would be a graduate student struggling to make ends meet. Cello couldn't be that popular. Certainly not like piano or, for pity's sake, the guitar.

I ransacked the internet, searching for an accomplished cellist who taught people of my ilk. Didn't I need a senior cello professional full of patience, depth of wisdom, and plenty of understanding to teach me? Someone special? Hadn't I earned that?

I fantasized the setting for great cello lessons might include the genteel experience of a private music studio. A lounge with Persian carpets to dampen the sound and to stick that metal spike out the bottom of the cello into. There would be a baby grand with the lid open, showing off the strings. Polite company to pass the time.

The search led to looking for cellists in the local symphony, many of whom had their own websites, although it turned out some maintained an elegant internet presence, while others hardly bothered. This search turned up a first chair cello player in the Oregon Symphony who appeared promising. She looked calm in her photo, and her credentials impeccable, so I sent a message. Explained I was an adult beginner looking for lessons, which prompted a quick response congratulating me for taking on the challenge and encouraging me onward. She sounded cordial, going on to explain she didn't give lessons and recommending I check with another cellist she named.

When I pinged that potential teacher, the person seemed a tad disorganized, even surprised to hear from a stranger asking for lessons, though she did teach. Her website looked trustworthy, if jumbled. She taught and performed, but when responding to my query, she got mixed up about what part of town I lived in and didn't manage to get back to me.

Another possible teacher responded after a delay, explaining how he taught in a church on the other side of town, an hour-long drive each way. That was if he could fit me into his schedule, which he didn't have currently updated but expected to soon. Behaving tiresomely, he finished by mentioning he had a GoFundMe page where people could make donations to buy him a cello. That had the ring of John Wayne riding into town without his hat.

I checked out as many other leads as I could find until, exhausted and dispirited, I began to feel as though this was a sign I'd begun a fool's journey. Until, in a moment of weakness, I emailed Lake Music, remembering their modest building a few blocks from my house, to ask if they offered cello lessons.

That evening a follow-up email arrived. "Yes, we do have a cello instructor here. Are you seeking lessons for yourself?" Tim, the owner, wrote.

I replied that I was.

Tim got right back to me. "Do you have a cello, or do you need to rent one?"

"I would need to rent a cello. I don't have one," I wrote back, letting it go at that.

Three days later Tim wrote me again. "Circling back on starting cello lessons. Let me know if you have any questions." During all the contacts I'd made with potential cello teachers, this was the only positive, problem-solving follow-up: Tim at Lake Music, the place I'd dismissed from the start.

I caved. We talked on the phone to clear up details about renting an instrument and how early in the day I could start, which was important because most students come in after school, so the evenings fill up. With nowhere else to go and a spark of interest from Lake Music, I signed up for a thirty-minute lesson once a week. The only information I had on the teacher was that she played the violin but also taught cello, bass, and piano—nothing more than these hints as to what I'd gotten myself into.

I'd taken other music lessons over the years on the trombone, guitar, and piano. Most stinging were the trombone lessons in high school, which I endured for one school year without any sign of improvement. A professor of music named Dr. Merle Hogg taught at the local college, San Diego State, and gave private trombone lessons on Saturday mornings. Hogg was a gangly man, had a good sense of humor, and you could tell, deeply enjoyed music.

He lived on the street at the bottom of the canyon below our house. To get to the lesson, I'd climb our back fence and, carrying my trombone, hike down through the sagebrush, around to the far side of the arroyo behind a row of houses, then follow along a drainage ditch to the Hogg residence. I either waited on the porch until the student ahead of me finished or went inside to hang out at the Hoggs' kitchen table while his kids made peanut butter sandwiches.

The trombone student taking the lesson before mine always played well, even performing duets with Hogg. The tone coming out of their horns sounded rich and clear and nuanced. They played actual songs rather than simple exercises and even discussed music theory.

My ability to get a big, rich tone out of the instrument never came to pass. I just didn't have the lips for it, I figured. Plus, I had the cheapest trombone my dad could dig out of the back closet at Thearle Music Company, the prominent music store of its day. I vividly remember him driving me to downtown San Diego in 1962 to purchase a Conn Director trombone. I must have been in fifth grade when the instrumental music program started up in our elementary school.

San Diego was much more of a Navy town at that time. Downtown, where several bases were located, was full of arcades jammed with sailors and marines. These and other distractions catered to servicemen—I don't recall ever seeing a woman in any of these places back then. These men were young and away from home for the first time, blowing off steam after completing basic training or returning from a deployment.

Some of the businesses were locker rooms with big hand-painted signs of cartoon sailors out front. Here, uniformed servicemen could change into civvies, have a good time—however painful the results— then uniform up again before returning to base.

I remember my father and I walking to the music store, seeing these places and looking into the window of one of many tattoo parlors. A young marine sat in a barber chair while his bare shoulder received artwork, quickly sobering up after a bout of poor decision-making. His eyes were wide and his face full of regret as he fully realized the painfully large caricature of a tough bulldog wearing a steel helmet and the words "USMC Devil Dogs" (or a similarly declarative caption) were being inked for eternity into his skin.

We seldom went downtown, so picking up that instrument, along with taking in this colorful activity, was another world. The excursion left a series of memorable impressions about things to avoid in the future.

I remember visiting the well-known Thearle Music Company for the first time—the first place I'd ever seen that sold nothing but musical instruments. The store had an old-fashioned layout with a vast area on the ground floor full of pianos. Everybody had a piano in their home back then. We even had my grandmother's ancient player piano in our garage. You pumped the piano's bellows with your feet, and a paper roll with a song punched into it played. I learned to sing along with "K-K-K-Katy" and other World War I-era tunes from the player piano rolls on this huge wooden box. I still know some of the lyrics: "When the m-m-m-moon shines over the c-c-c-cow shed, I'll be waiting at the k-k-k-kitchen door."

We climbed the stairs to a wide balcony, an alcove full of brass instruments.

As if they knew each other, my dad said to the sales clerk, "The trombone."

An obvious setup. Dad had clearly been down there to make arrangements in advance. There was no discussion with me about it. Just, this is what you're getting.

Simple as that, the clerk pulled out a cheap trombone considered a student model. He opened the case to show me the instrument, which unscrewed in the middle and was stored in two parts. This trombone didn't have the look of a well-crafted metal instrument. Other kids playing trombone owned better models, some with two-colored metal that held a shine, had a larger bell, and produced better sound. I didn't receive an explanation. They didn't show me any of these other models, certainly none of the expensive ones I would have preferred, nor did they give me a tour of the place.

For having only been in the fifth grade, I remember a lot of detail about the whole thing. I sensed I'd missed an important musical milestone. I suppose I should have recognized going to this store as unusual enough, because my father actually spent money on me. Like so many parents in the post-WWII decades who grew up during the Great Depression, he unendingly feared being broke. Anything costing more than fifty dollars was a blur to him. For my dad to buy me even the cheapest student trombone meant putting a crowbar in his wallet to pry it open. He acted, in some strange way, like he'd been robbed. Kids pick up on this sort of thing. This behavior colors events and hangs on for a lifetime.

However bad a trombone player I was, how much can I blame the trombone I got for not being a comfortable, easy-to-play instrument? Or for the instrument's and my inability to produce a robust and pleasing sound?

During one lesson, Dr. Hogg wanted me to produce a better tone. He had me open my jaw behind my buzzing lips, to the point my teeth were off the mouthpiece, in an attempt to improve the sound I produced. Playing with my mouth this wide was impossible, of course, but I made the effort, which left me feeling even more incapable of playing well.

"How much do you practice?" Hogg asked with the knowledge the answer was obviously little.

"Not enough," I admitted.

"If you don't practice, you might as well take the three dollars your parents pay for this lesson and flush them down the toilet." Hogg held up the three one-dollar bills I'd given him. "You have to practice to improve."

He was right about this. I didn't enjoy playing the trombone—at least not this trombone—so why practice? I kept hearing how lousy I played, so there wasn't any reason to continue lessons after the end of that school year.

Chapter 3
No Prophet

On an autumn afternoon a couple of weeks after I'd returned from Spain, I pulled into the weedy parking lot of Lake Music for my first cello lesson. The building is located in Lake Oswego, Oregon, on Boones Ferry Road, which was originally a pioneer dirt track leading to a ferry boat, trailblazed by Alphonso Boone, a grandson of the imperfectly remembered pioneer Daniel Boone. These little bits of history I find fascinating, however little they had to do with my musical progress.

Lake Music shared an old flat-roofed, concrete-block building with Casa del Pollo, a Costa Rican restaurant. At the *tico* end of the building—*tico* being a friendly name Costa Ricans call themselves—were festive flags, travel posters, and the alluring smells of the ceviche served on Fridays and Saturdays. Soccer matches played perpetually on a big-screen TV.

On the musical end of the building, things were more sedate. The side of the Lake Music building facing the busy street was painted with giant piano keys, about two octaves' worth of black and white rectangles. On the business side, where the front entrance faces the parking lot, the aluminum-framed door proved especially hard to push open. The few windows along this stretch of wall were covered with makeshift metal grilles, suggesting the genteel incarceration of music students.

Setting aside my scorching recollection of past musical failure, I pushed open the door. Inside, a threadbare carpet formed a green pool on the floor. A wandering linoleum path snaked around the room, revealing two tired-looking cellos hung up high where little kids couldn't reach. Two string basses on the floor stood like mountains with "Do Not Touch" signs on them. The far wall displayed a high school band's worth of clarinets, a French horn, trumpets—always a popular choice—along with flutes and a sax.

A sheet music rack held a selection of violin books, a few for cello, and maybe one or two for viola. Teaching books for woodwinds and brass, guitar, and everything else were tucked around the other side of a drum set over by some electric pianos. Budget guitars hung like unpicked fruit, both on a distant wall and from the rack in the middle of the room. A bouquet of ukuleles painted with Hawaiian motifs illuminated a distant corner, adding a splash of color to an otherwise dreary decor. They sell a lot of ukes, I was told.

Several plastic containers were placed around the room to catch drips from the leaky roof. The wall above the register had a vast swatch of brown paint flaking off the wall due to these problems. Word was that a plan existed to fix the roof and update the building. Tim had taken over the business from his father. Ran it while earning a living teaching tennis. He also played a lot of pickleball and competed in tournaments.

Three steps inside, a woman sitting at the front counter said, "You're my new student. I'm Mary Ann. I'm minding the store until the regular guy gets in."

Mary Ann brandished a massive shock of thick white hair, cut straight across her shoulders and parted down the middle. This might have been the thickest crop of hair I have ever seen. The impressive mane framed a face that could easily belong to a six-term senator or a noted philosopher.

"I'm seventy-one. I guess pretty old to be starting cello—way older than most of your students," I said.

"I'm seventy-seven, so there," Mary Ann replied with a breezy smile. "I teach all ages. My youngest student is two. He wants to be an orchestra conductor."

"That's pretty young," I replied, wondering how Mary Ann managed four different kinds of instruments and what sort of background brought her to Lake Music. "You teach other instruments, too?"

"Violin's my primary instrument," she explained.

"Interesting. I wondered who my teacher would be," I said.

The regular clerk arrived, so Mary Ann led me back to a narrow corridor that ran along the front of the store. These were the small rooms with grated windows you could see from out front.

"This is my teaching studio. It's small and cramped. Freezing cold too. I'm going to turn on the heater." The smallest space heater ever made sat on the floor in the corner. It was the size of a toaster but produced less heat.

To get a feel for the dimensions of this studio, think of the smallest closet in the crummiest apartment you've ever lived in. Cram into that space a storage box of Mary Ann's papers, an adjustable music stand, two chairs, and a backless stool, which is preferred by string players who, I suppose, pride themselves on good posture. Then add a cello, cello case, a student, and the teacher.

Mary Ann's studio walls were papered with concert announcements, fingerboard charts, handwritten messages about persistence, rules listing reasons to stay home when sick, and what to do about missed lessons, lending the place an edifying presentiment.

"I leave the door open to get some air in here," Mary Ann said, settling into the wooden chair to my left. "It's noisy, but we need to breathe."

I sat in the chair by the door, hemmed in by the music stand in front of me and my rental instrument in its case, which leaned in the corner.

"How about you unpack your cello," she said.

I opened the case and freed the instrument from an internal strap without damaging it. We slid the empty case out the door, where it took up most of the corridor.

I'd seen these instruments plenty of times, but never had any reason to touch a living, breathing cello. The thing that immediately struck me about the instrument was how light it was for all its size. Lifting the cello took little effort, because a cello is a wooden balloon with a neck small enough to get your whole hand around.

"How familiar are you with the cello?" Mary Ann asked.

"First time I've ever held one. It's remarkably light. Seems fragile," I said.

"They're stronger than they look," she assured me. "The design is hundreds of years old."

The cello weighed all of eight pounds, about the same as a gallon of milk. I confirmed this on a digital bathroom scale when I got home. Still, the instrument felt so delicate, I was afraid I'd bang a hole in it or even break the thing apart before my lesson ended. Logically, you pick up the cello by the neck, though when moving the instrument around, it wanted to bump into the music stand, the corner of the chair—every edge and hard surface it came near.

Mary Ann showed me how to extend the endpin from the bottom, which raised the instrument off the floor so I could steady it between my knees and play. A simple thumbscrew loosened and tightened the hold. I'd heard it called a "spike" because it has a sharp point, but "endpin," Mary Ann explained, is the proper name.

This began the seemingly endless process of sliding the endpin in and out to determine how high or low the cello needed to be for me to play effectively. Does the cello go on top of one knee then rest on the inside of the other? What was too high, and when did the position get too low to play? Accidently shifting the spot where the endpin stuck into the carpet changed the cello's angle and height far more than I imagined it would.

This went on for a while until I found a position that worked for the moment. Only then did I pluck the fattest, deepest sounding string to hear how the cello sounded. Compared to the guitar, the only other stringed instrument I had ever played, the note sounded huge. The body of the instrument gently vibrated.

"You're a violin player, you said?" I asked, and Mary Ann replied affirmatively.

"Cello, too?" I continued.

Mary Ann smiled warmly. "I was a violinist with the Oregon Symphony Orchestra for forty-two years and the first female symphony orchestra manager in the US," she said.

"You were?" I leaned back in my chair, fumbling to keep the cello upright.

"Cello's my second instrument. I studied violin and cello in college while getting a degree in musical performance," she explained.

Mary Ann Coggins Kaza was a calm, talented professional and a peer with vast reservoirs of life and music experience. In fact, Mary Ann had been the wife of a well-known local musician, conductor, and educator. She was deeply connected throughout the musical community.

She went on. "I've performed with Yo-Yo Ma, Rostropovich, Zara Nelsova, Lenny Bernstein ..." Yes, she referred to Leonard Bernstein as "Lenny." "... Henry Mancini, Itzhak Perlman, Barbra Streisand, Doc Severinsen, Tony Bennett, and a load of other classical and contemporary musicians and conductors. Oh, and I've played Carnegie

Hall," she added. "I was in Lake Music six years ago buying violin strings—I like to buy local—their violin teacher had just quit, and they asked if I wanted to teach," she explained, seated comfortably across from me. "Been here ever since."

Hooly dooly on a cracker, I thought. The cello teacher I'd been looking for had been hiding in plain sight, ensconced in the music shop beside a Costa Rican restaurant, waiting for me to stumble in asking for lessons. She was lurking here all this time? I'd been looking in the wrong places. A cello teacher with this experience was just around the corner from where I live, after I'd resisted the place. What's the other quote? "No prophet is accepted in his own hometown."

My lack of common sense caused me to suppose an affable instructor with a boatload of experience couldn't be unearthed a few blocks from my house.

"Let's start with the parts of the cello to acquaint you with it." Mary Ann began at the top of the instrument where the wood curled around on itself. "The scroll is a traditional figure, the design of which is based on a nautilus. It's the standard decoration. It sits on top of the peg box, where the tuning pegs stick out. However, some old instruments are more ornate. Sometimes they will have a lion's head or even a dragon on them."

From there, we worked down the cello to the four tuning pegs fit into holes in the peg box. These pegs can be turned to tune each string.

Mary Ann didn't stick with one topic, though her jumping around was fine with me. I didn't stick with a single topic either. She talked about her rebuilt knees and how they made holding the cello difficult. Because she taught a lot of kids, she wore T-shirts with dinosaurs and comic book monsters with unbuttoned long-sleeve shirts over them. Her jeans were covered with sparkles all around the bottoms of the legs. "I dress like this to keep the kids relaxed and interested."

Mary Ann seemed like she'd be a natural sitting at a campfire telling true-life stories, playing a fiddle while the trail crew slapped their hands together, hooting and hollering. She was a violin player first, after all. As Mary Ann pointed to parts of the cello, I could see her hands gave testimony to decades of playing the violin.

On a commercial communications assignment early in my freelance days, I wrote the script and interviewed farmers for a short film celebrating the fiftieth anniversary of the Cenex Co-op. "Where the customer is the company" was its slogan at the time. I interviewed several working farmers from the North Dakota and Minnesota prairies in a film studio.

All these folks had worked outside their entire lives, grabbing, throwing, shoving, lifting, and moving heavy, awkward loads, and their hands showed their toil. A younger farmer in his mid-forties had developed muscular fingers from the strain and exercise of grasping and hauling all day. While filming his interview, he sat calmly on the couch, his hands resting palms down, one on the other. He told story after story about his career on the family farm. Working outside in weather, exercising all day long. Using his hands every day, day after day.

Similarly, Mary Ann's hands were powerful. Every knuckle distinct, lean, with experienced fingers and blunt fingertips, callused on the left hand from pressing on steel strings while moving them quickly and accurately in time with the music. Her hands told stories.

"The tuning pegs, one for each string. You turn them to adjust the pitch. They only get looser, never tighter over time." She leaned toward the instrument, pointing out the two pegs on each side. "Each peg is tapered so it has a pressure fit, wood to wood. When the weather changes, they'll likely come loose. Might even fall out—happens all the time. One young student's tuning pegs all fell out last time the weather changed, and the bridge collapsed," Mary Ann explained. "The mother called, and I told her it wasn't the student's fault."

She pointed to the bridge—the flat piece of carved wood holding up the strings between the nut at the top of the ebony fingerboard—and the tail piece, the narrow black board at the bottom of the cello. Then Mary Ann explained the C-bouts, the curved indentations at the waist of the cello. "These are inset so the bow doesn't hit the body of the instrument as it reaches across the string. They also help reinforce the instrument. The round top of the cello is the upper bout, and the curved bottom, the lower bout. How 'bout that?"

"Ha," I said.

She went on to run through the other high points of the instrument. In front, the F-holes, so named for their shape, provide an opening to let out sound toward the audience. Each is marked with notches indicating where to place the bridge.

Next, Mary Ann talked about the fine tuners, the four screws at the top of the tail piece, used to micro-adjust the pitch.

I had roughly set the height of the cello by lengthening the endpin, but Mary Ann delivered a thorough explanation anyway. "On the bottom of the cello, an endpin slides in and out. It's adjusted to hold the cello at the best height for the individual cellist," she explained. "Let's have a look."

I turned the cello onto its back, resting it on my lap. By loosening the thumbscrew securing the endpin, I slid the endpin out about a foot, then retightened the screw to hold it in place.

When I turned the cello upright again, it stood between my knees, and I began the awkward process of getting the damn thing into a workable position to play. No matter how wide or narrow I held my knees, the cello kept moving around. I tried raising and lowering the endpin and moving the point where the endpin stuck into the carpet without finding any equilibrium. Positioning a cello is an ongoing compromise between cello and cellist.

Now that I had a passing familiarity with the parts of the cello and had it vertical, Mary Ann invited me to hold the bow. Not to make a sound on a string, just to hold the bow in my hand.

My rental cello came with a bow, which I took by the handle the way I'd hold a framing hammer. The bow waved around like a sword, seemingly on its own, making me afraid of stabbing my new teacher.

"The end you're holding is the frog," she said.

"The frog," I echoed.

"Nobody knows why it's called that."

"All the more reason to call it the frog," I said.

"The pointy tip on the end is obviously called the tip." She pointed to the parts of the bow, going on to explain how complicated the frog design is. There's a U-shaped notch, a screw to tighten or loosen the hair stretched from one end to the other. The bow has a classic shape achieved through a great deal of experimentation several hundred years ago.

"The long, curved part is the stick or shaft. These are traditionally wood," Mary Ann explained. "However, the wood that's used is an endangered Brazilian hardwood. Bow makers have shifted to a bow made of composite materials, usually graphite." My loaner bow was one of these lightweight, strong, reinforced-plastic bows that can be manufactured with varying degrees of flexibility and tinted to look like wood. I could have been told the bow was wood and thought nothing of it.

"Okay, now," Mary Ann began.

In my experience, if someone begins an explanation with "Okay, now," something difficult, complicated, or uncomfortable comes next.

"What?"

"This is how you hold the bow." She took the bow, holding the frog by drooping her index, middle, ring, and pinky fingers over the front. Her thumb mysteriously disappeared on the other side, somehow getting tucked into the U-shaped notch. You're not exactly holding or grasping the bow, but cooperating with it.

"Your first finger," Mary Ann said. I realized for the first time that fingers are numbered when you play the cello, and she was referring to my index finger. "Is used to press down the bow, to apply pressure to the tip."

I didn't get what all that meant. Applying pressure to the tip from the other end of the bow required further investigation.

I tried to organize my four fingers over the frog correctly, then took a stab at positioning my thumb so it made sense dealing with the small U opening, which had a stabbing square corner.

When learning to play golf years before, my golf teacher, who has an easy name to remember, Pete Julsrud, worked through all sorts of maneuvers to get me to hit the ball straight. Most made no sense on their own. This included making your head the center of the swinging circle, keeping your left wrist and arm straight while rotating the club face up on the drawback, and hitting down on the ball. Getting the golf grip right has spawned an entire industry of helpful devices and ceaseless instruction.

Same thing getting my thumb properly into the U-shaped notch in the frog, letting the bow balance itself on the strings, and learning that bounce in a bow is a good thing. The bow is not a wild animal you should have to wrestle to control.

"Do this," Mary Ann showed me. "Place your thumb in that slot. Keep the knuckle of your thumb bent. If you hold your thumb straight, it will cramp up on you."

I'd heard of medieval thumbscrews and wondered if the cello bow had been perfected at about the same time. Once she got my hand in the right orientation, Mary Ann took a photo of both sides of my grip for reference.

Holding a hissing, writhing snake is more natural than correctly grasping a cello bow for the first time.

"You'll get used to it. It'll become effortless for you to work with the bow this way," Mary Ann said reassuringly.

"Feels like I'm going to drop it," I said.

"Trust me on this," she said with quiet determination.

Professional cellists seem to play relaxed and with such pleasure, their cello comfortably resting on the endpin and their sternum. With their knees steadying the whole thing, the bow flies to just the right places. Easy as pie, I thought.

Not so. Playing a cello is an act of continuous negotiation with the instrument.

Mary Ann threw herself into teaching with plenty of zeal, keeping the momentum going. Swiftly moving from one topic to another. Everything a surprise.

We used up the half-hour lesson getting the instrument out of the case, setting it up, and gaining some initial understanding about the bow, with Mary Ann taking pictures along the way. I could use the photos she took of me holding the bow correctly, for a hot minute, to duplicate where my fingers went and how the cello and I sat in the chair.

"Try it," May Ann said.

"For real?" I pulled the bow across a string, hearing a lugubrious tone resonate from the thickest string. I had nothing to compare the sound against. It didn't have the screechy squeal of an amateur, at least not yet. I tried the other strings, then two at a time.

"Put your finger on that line and play the C string, the one closest to you," Mary Ann said.

I eyed a plastic strip stuck across the fingerboard that marked the first full step up the scale. It was one of the temporary markings on the fingerboard to help the student learn where to press the strings. Since this was a rental instrument and had been used by legions of beginners for years, the cello sported dings, the occasional bruise, and wear in odd spots. It also had both the first position and fourth position marked, the fingerboard amiss with the remains of sticky dots, all of these hints to where to find the note you're hunting for.

Unlike guitar and banjo players who use thin raised metal ridges marking every note for them, cello fingerboards are bald as a billiard ball.

We went over a simple scale, and I scratched out "Twinkle, Twinkle, Little Star."

"I have everybody play 'Twinkle' during their first lesson. It shows them that they can play a tune right away," she said.

We went into overtime on this first lesson. The next student waited in the hallway on a hard bench for Mary Ann to finish.

"Here's a book to start with." She placed a cello book for adult beginners in my hand. "You know how to read music, so you have a major advantage starting out," she said, then gave me an assignment. "Work on positioning your cello so it's comfortable. Work on grasping the frog by looking at the photos I sent you to find the correct finger positions. Practice with the bow to get a feel for playing. Use the entire bow, not just a small part of the hair on the bow. Lastly, check out the book, just to begin familiarizing yourself with it."

Mary Ann followed me out into the store, reviewing what she hoped I'd absorbed.

"You learned to grasp the bow today. How to position the cello. You couldn't do that before you came in here," she said while her next student got situated.

"Right, thanks," I said. Part of me felt afraid of never being able to master this instrument, even modestly.

"See you next week," she said.

As I shoved the cello into the back of my car, I felt I might have been visited, for a moment, by another angel unawares. At least I found a guide to get started.

Chapter 4
Under the Dashboard of My Car

When I got home from my first lesson, I left the cello in its case and put the case in the living room, between the dining table and the fireplace we never use. I'm leery of fireplaces in houses. All those stories about embers getting on the carpet and burning down the house scare me.

A few hours later, Susan returned home from her part-time job at a winery and found herself gazing at a cello case she'd never seen before. There was no way to disguise it.

I had neglected to tell Susan about my wanton determination to learn the cello. Certainly, other husbands have worse obsessions, such as building a hot rod in the garage or buying a small plane in parts and taking years to assemble the thing.

The expense never concerned me. If learning the cello was a hobby, the cost was modest compared to, say, restoring an antique boat or regularly playing golf at a private course. Scuba diving required a bigger cash outlay for the equipment, training, and travel. In fact, when scuba diving caught my attention, I took enough courses to earn several specialties, including ice driving, which I passed in Lake Minnetonka during a Minnesota January. I wound up flying to Australia and diving the Great Barrier Reef. All this totaled up to a fair chunk of change, far more than I expected my desire to play the cello would cost.

Many other hobbies cost a lot more and would require advanced notice, I figured. There is something inherently soothing about having a wooden instrument in the house, so it's not that bad having one unexpectedly show up in your living room.

At least that was the assumption I was going on.

Adding to the scenery, I'd retrieved a music stand from the garage that had been gathering cobwebs since I'd given up on the guitar. I kept the music stand after I sold my Fender American Deluxe Telecaster—much as I loved everything about the instrument, I simply did not play it.

Somehow, I knew music would orbit back into my life, so rather than selling or donating the stand, I stuck it on a garage shelf to wait for the musical urge to return.

"What's that?" Susan asked, two notches above "Oh, that's interesting."

"My cello," I said. "Don't worry, I didn't buy it."

"Why do you have a cello you didn't buy?" Susan asked, as if curious why I'd brought home broccolini rather than broccoli.

"I need it to practice between lessons," I said. Hadn't she experienced a moment of enlightenment in Spain, too?

"Cello lessons?" Susan asked.

"Remember the Spanish guy, the cellist who played for us in Spain?" I asked.

"What about him?"

"I'd like to play the way he does. Didn't you think he was compelling?"

"Cello?" she said flatly.

I assured Susan I was only taking cello lessons at Lake Music, not anywhere special or expensive. Surely there was no danger in that, was there? Our kids took music lessons there, and they turned out all right. It didn't keep them from becoming fully employed or anything major.

In an attempt to generate interest and create a positive aura around the idea of having a cello in the house, I took it out of its case to demonstrate what I'd learned from my first lesson. The student cello had all the stickers marking finger positions. It showed its age and looked like it'd been dragged around the block a couple times. I pulled it over to a hardwood dining chair, sat, and placed the cello onto my lap to loosen the thumb screw, then pulled the steel pin out about a foot.

Every time I thought I'd adjusted the cello to a good angle, the endpin would slip on the floor. The tip of the endpin was sharp, which worked well on the teaching studio's carpeted floor, but scratched our maple floor like the wood had been clawed by a mountain lion.

The endpin did come with a removable rubber tip, which I kept on the end at first. Sadly, it didn't grip the wood well with or without the tip on. I'd tend to this later. For now, I grasped the frog of the bow that came with the student cello and pulled the horsehair across the C string. What sounded to me like a great, magnificent note rang out.

Susan appeared not to notice my elegant note. How it vibrated. The way the sound rang, lingering long after I lifted the bow from the string. I had learned that second-generation Norwegians from small towns on the Mississippi, such as her hometown of La Crosse, Wisconsin, never seem to show exuberance about much of anything. At least not so I could tell.

"How long are you going to do this?" she asked, puzzled.

"Just trying it out," I explained, adding I could quit anytime since I was just renting the cello and might run out of steam.

Susan seemed to accept my explanation without any additional follow-up questions and left to find something else to do.

That evening, I studied the picture Mary Ann took of my hand correctly grasping the frog. Over and over, I played a few notes with the bow, then adjusted the position of my fingers to better approximate the correct position. Your thumb should provide a balancing point to easily let the bow work with the cello. Instead, my thumb on one side and fingers on the other fumbled the bow out of my hand, sending it clanking to the floor.

This experimentation continued throughout the week, leading to my second lesson. I spent hours exploring different sounds a cello could produce and the best way to hold the bow. I yearned for the cello to suddenly stop fighting and accept me.

The most celebrated cellist on earth is Yo-Yo Ma. The famous black-and-white film of a young Ma playing cello with Leonard Bernstein and the New York Philharmonic is astonishing. His family moved from China to Paris, where he was born, then to New York. He started performing at four-and-a-half, showing great aptitude for the cello from the beginning.

Ma plays all over the world, including performing at President Barack Obama's inauguration and other high-profile events with symphonies, solo shows, chamber music–size groups.

I started watching Yo-Yo Ma videos to understand the basics—for starters, how he holds the cello. Where he positions his feet, where the tuning pegs are in relation to his head, how he pushes and pulls the bow across the strings in relation to the bridge and end of the fingerboard. Are his fingers bent or straight, or in some particular combination as he made string crossings?

How does Ma play the cello? I saw his feet stay flat on the floor, and he doesn't tap a foot to the music. It's okay to tap your foot if you're playing jazz, I guess, but not the cello. His expression is neutral or dreamy, as if he's carried away with the music. Sometimes he plays with his eyes closed, periodically turning his head to the side and tipping it toward the balcony.

Ultimately, everything Ma does to create a compelling performance is present when you study him playing. There are hundreds of Yo-Yo Ma performances available for viewing online from multiple sources. I binge watched dozens of them in a matter of days.

I pushed furniture aside to practice, staking out a cello zone into the space between our round dining table and the living room. This provided enough space to station the cello so I could easily slide over a dining table chair and play when the mood struck.

At the far corner of the living room was a silver York E-flat tuba resting on its bell. Purchased years ago, the tuba is solely decorative, despite the fact that I had an instrument repair professional polish it and get the valves working once. I never played it. The annual Tuba Christmas Concert in many cities brings enthusiasts from all over town together, and without ever participating, I found myself on their mailing list. How did they find out I have a tuba?

I thought a nice addition to my decorative instrument collection would be a double-bell euphonium, a wild-looking horn with two bells. The double-bell euphonium first came to my attention when sung about in *The Music Man* as one of many instruments Professor Harold Hill sold to the parents in River City, Iowa. I've often thought one of these hung on the wall would add to the decor.

The time between my urge to begin studying the cello and the moment I took my first lesson, then having a cello at home, was fast and effortless, without any reflection about my motives. I just wanted to find out if whatever that warm sense of fulfillment the Spaniard had shown us from the cello was possible to recreate.

After a week of attempting to play a cello, I wondered if this alone was what was driving me and why the deep and sudden determination.

At that, I began to consider the whole of my musical journey, since I first remember marching around the house to phonograph records playing classical symphonies when I was a youngster. Who can sit still during the *William Tell Overture* when you're a little kid? It's the soundtrack to so many old cartoons. You get up and march around the room in time with the music without anyone explaining how. It's built into all of us.

What did I most delight in about music? If I came to terms with where the depth of that enjoyment came from, would it help explain how listening to a cello one odd evening on a trip to Spain rocketed me into this musical spot? Propelled me to find a cello teacher? Did I have a musical experience I could look back on to help me understand what led me here?

Later that afternoon, when I sat down with this rental cello and pulled the bow across a string, I realized when that moment might have been.

I had squeezed underneath the dashboard of my 1964 Volvo 122S. This gray station wagon was made in Sweden with red leather seats, manual choke, over-the-shoulder seatbelts, and a four-speed transmission. The engine generated eighty-four horsepower. It was my first car.

At the time, everybody wanted to upgrade the standard AM radio to something more glorious, so I decided to install a cassette player myself. All my friends were upgrading their systems this way, using a screwdriver, pliers, wire cutters—everybody was doing it.

After rummaging around under the dash for a while, I cut holes in the door panels to install new speakers. The wires seemed to go in the right places, and the cassette player screwed into the bottom of the dash after some wrestling around. As a test, I pushed a cassette tape I'd just bought into the slot, the Beatles' brand-new album *Abbey Road*.

"Here Comes the Sun," a song I had never heard before, began to play.

The lead-in has a long, descending note at the end. With my head between the stereo speakers under the dash, I listened to this note move from the left speaker to the right speaker—what a moment. This was as high tech as you could get at the time. Stereo. Big stuff. Electronics were beginning to make huge improvements, great leaps in how we listened to music.

I was eighteen, just out of high school, and realized how important music was to everyone in the world at the height of Beatlemania. It was also 1969, the summer of love, or at least one of the summers of love. We landed on the moon. The Vietnam War raged on, while young men my age, my friends, were drafted and sent away. Our leaders were being gunned down. All of society seemed in turmoil. For me, 1969 was the year I began college, and I was listening to the Beatles full blast, selling hamburgers at the Safari Kitchen in the world-famous San Diego Zoo, and trying to make sense of everything.

That "Here Comes the Sun," head-under-the-dashboard moment became the perfect tune at just the right time to be stamped in my brain. Could I someday manage to get good enough to play "Here Comes the Sun" on a cello to celebrate that moment? Would it create a new musical highlight moment all these years later?

The Beatles were a sudden, dazzling comet captivating hearts and minds during those years, resonating with the existential yearning of youth. Each song brimmed with emotion, storytelling, the transformational spirit of that moment. For me, they arrived at the height of the Vietnam War when I became eligible for the draft in the midst of a world of social unrest. I didn't understand what was going on, but the Beatles seemed to understand, at least well enough to turn it into music, which made it all the more powerful.

They inspired a wave of creativity and social consciousness that continues to resonate. We will be talking about them until the end of time.

I had the notion to learn to play "Here Comes the Sun" both to recreate that musical moment under the dashboard of my Volvo and perhaps because George Harrison was the only Beatle I hadn't crossed paths with. Harrison wasn't easy to catch in a concert over the years as he didn't perform much. He died when only fifty-eight years old, having first recorded with the group when only nineteen. I'd always wanted to see him but never did.

The other Beatles I had stumbled across, two of them by accident.

Paul McCartney performed with his band Wings in Saint Paul, Minnesota. When I lived there, I was able to get tickets to the packed concert. Paul's wife, Linda, sat in with the band, playing the piano and singing. Plenty of people talked about her being there, snarkily wondering if her piano and microphone were even plugged in. McCartney played a two-hour set that night without breaking a sweat, creating a comfortable, personalized feel to the show. Of course, there was a moment when a single chair was placed downstage, in the blaze of a spotlight, for "Michelle."

For one year after college, I lived in New York City. I'd just graduated with a degree in theater arts, and a few friends were in Manhattan studying dance, so I joined them there. This was in 1974 and 1975. I found a three-dollar-an-hour job in the McGraw Hill Bookstore on Sixth Avenue. Shared an apartment with a fellow named Leon Schmidt. My half of the rent ran $145, which I could barely scrape together each month on my microscopic salary in pricey New York.

Our apartment sat on West 84th Street, half a block off Central Park. I jogged in the park, walked over to the Guggenheim, and snuck into theaters to see the second act of big-ticket shows I couldn't afford. A quick walk south of my apartment sat The Dakota, the distinguished building where John Lennon lived with his wife, Yoko Ono.

Lennon strolled around this part of Manhattan freely. Photos of this era show him wearing an "I Heart NY" T-shirt, often a hat, always round glasses and bell-bottom jeans.

I would see Lennon on the street, alone or taking a breezy stroll with Yoko, wearing that shirt. Once he joined a demonstration to end the Vietnam War taking place in Central Park, in an opening not far from The Dakota. The grassy area was full of people, and when I happened onto it, I climbed up on a boulder by the path where I came in and stood there above the crowd to see what was going on.

Seeing a celebrity at a peace rally during the Vietnam War shouldn't have been a surprise. But as John Lennon strolled in right by my big rock, the crowd fell silent. It seemed like make-believe when he appeared. You could not get more famous than John Lennon, and here he seemed to appear out of thin air.

He talked about peace and concluded his remarks by asking that people "Just let me walk out, would you, please." People opened a passage for him without a word. He strolled unimpeded by fans, right past me again. I looked down to watch the top of his head go by, wondering if I ought to reach out and shake his hand, but didn't.

I ran into Lennon again, ran straight into him, maybe a month or so later. Leaving a movie theater in our neighborhood, I pushed on the lobby door to exit as someone on the outside pulled it open. We ran full body smack into each other, throwing us both off balance.

"Ow, 'scuse me," the man exclaimed.

"Sorry," I replied, not fully realizing at first who I'd slammed into until I turned to see the Beatle go inside with a couple of friends.

On my first trip to New Zealand, we had a two-night stopover in Fiji and stayed in a resort hotel in Nadi. This was one of the trips I took with my friend Chris Berne and the first day we had the afternoon to wander. A thirty-minute walk took us to the downtown business district, where shops sold traditional wood carvings and local crafts.

After a little looking around, Chris and I headed back to the hotel, climbing the long grade to the entrance. The open lobby spread out in front under the tropical sun. No doors or walls, only a broad roof protecting the front desk from the heat and an occasional afternoon shower. We were about fifty yards away when I saw the figure of a compact man walking between a taxi parked at the far side of the lot and the lobby desk.

At this distance, the distinctive long strides of the figure's short legs, the shape of the silhouette, the long hair and moustache registered. Hadn't I seen a cartoon character with the same walk and outline in the *Yellow Submarine* animated movie?

"That's Ringo Starr," I said to Chris as we approached.

"No, it's not," Chris said, keeping our walking pace steady.

"That's Ringo."

"No, it's not," Chris replied with more certainty until we took a few more paces and he adjusted his glasses. "That is Ringo."

We continued to a wall on the far side of the parking area. There we stood with dumbfounded stares as Ringo approached the expansive outdoor reception desk, finished checking out, and walked back in front of us again. He headed back to his taxi where his wife, Barbara Bach, waited. She was recognizable, a Bond girl from the 007 film *The Spy Who Loved Me*, among other films, and *Playboy* Playmate of the Month centerfold.

It's worth remembering that Bach met Ringo when they co-stared in the 1981 film *Caveman*. The dialogue of this movie is made up of grunts creating a pretend caveman language. A highlight of the film is when a T-Rex gets stoned.

Chapter 5
A Branch of May

The thread of my musical journey began in Miss Rixman's choral music class. Choir, my first organized musical experience, took place in a dedicated music room and involved more than simply knocking sticks together to make rhythms. Each of our elementary school grades sang songs that we performed in a program for our parents under the direction of Miss Rixman.

When we met her, Miss Rixman was a successful midcareer choral instructor, who went on to get her doctorate in music education. On top of running primary school music programs, she organized her own ensemble, The Rixman Choral, which performed around town.

Like so many teachers of the era, she ruled with discipline rather than finding softer, more enlightened, and compassionate strategies to moderate student behavior. She wanted her elementary grade singers to follow directions, stand quietly for hours—we never sat at choir rehearsals or for performances—and insisted on other constraints primary school kids struggle with. She came across as stern and unhappy—but determined to make us enjoy music. Force us if necessary.

I certainly couldn't stand still, but I had a good ear, sang on pitch, and was extroverted enough to belt out a song in front of an audience. Amazingly, Miss Rixman said I sang well enough to be in the Vienna Boys' Choir. No kidding. A great compliment from her—she felt I could hit the right notes and sounded that clear. A popular Disney movie at the time was *Almost Angels* about the Vienna Boys' Choir, which probably sparked the comparison.

Miss Rixman picked me to sing a solo, backed up by the rest of the sixth-graders. The song was "A Branch of May," a traditional folksong about giving someone a twig from a tree. A couple of lines I remember go "A branch of May I give to you ..." followed by "It is but a sprout but well budded out." Getting picked to do this seemed special, whatever my voice quality may have been at the time.

Decades later, our elementary school class got together for reunions, as we had all grown from nursery school to kindergarten all the way through sixth grade together, and some of us went on through secondary school and even college together. We talked about our teachers and looked up Miss Rixman. We found her ashes entombed in a columbarium at a church in San Diego's Mission Valley. She shared a niche in the church wall with another woman. The inscription read "Dr. Eunice Rixman."

"Miss Rixman, you were ahead of your time, and we didn't know it," we said when we saw the inscription.

There were other early attempts at improving my music education at this age.

Around fourth grade, I found myself taking piano lessons from a woman named Mrs. Plazick at her house. She was a lean, preoccupied woman. I learned to read music in her living room. She put stars on the individual exercises in a beginner book as I completed them. These lessons were a halfhearted attempt by my parents to get me to play piano and stopped after they got tired of driving me.

A more important step in my musical journey came when my class reached fifth grade. Our teacher announced, "We're going to the music department today so you can pick an instrument. You're all going to be in a band."

A band?

Our elementary school was on the San Diego State College campus, the school's name later upgraded to university. Student teachers would visit our classes to watch us learn and were sometimes assigned for a semester to our grade. We were accustomed to being in a sea of college students. For band class, we ambled across campus to the old music building. Its disorderly layout of rooms smelled of valve oil and sheet music as we climbed the stairs.

Inside, most of the rooms didn't have windows to allow the ensembles to practice without the danger of being heard. Music stands and chairs were scattered all over. We heard trumpets and pianos and saxophones playing, but we couldn't see them as we walked down the halls. This gave the space and music an eerie vibe. Was this what learning about music would be like?

The two dozen of us were led into a storage room crammed full of instruments loaned to students for classes, many worse for wear. A music teacher we'd never seen before explained the different instruments.

"This is a clarinet. It is a woodwind." His name was Mr. Biggs. He was a thin little guy with a big head. Wore brown pants with a crease, a white shirt, and a tie with a pattern that looked like tree bark. "On this side are the brass instruments." He held up a French horn, the instrument he played.

A big bass drum on a stand dominated the room from where I was standing. During a subsequent visit to this room, while waiting for class to start, I beat on this drum and broke a hole in it. This caused some turmoil, but the drum was old and I was in fifth grade. When questioned about damaging the drum, I advised them, "Everybody bangs that drum."

Mr. Biggs looked down at me. "People rob banks. Does that mean you should rob banks, too?"

I never much liked him after that. This experience also taught me that music involves a lot of interaction with other people, some of it highly structured and with a hierarchy. Though playing music outside a classroom can ultimately have as much or as little structure as the musician wants.

They handed out instruments. There were a couple string instruments available for students, but playing one never occurred to me because you couldn't join a marching band with a violin or string bass. I knew marching band was a high school thing, and I needed to be ready when I got there.

"What're you going to play?" I asked my friends.

"I'm playing trombone," Phil Frye announced. Phil proved himself a good authority on most matters and provided me with helpful older-brother-style advice over the years. "My brother played trombone, so I'm going to play trombone."

I said, "Then I'm going to play trombone too."

The trombone they gave me had a good hundred-thousand miles on it. A college student from the music department showed me how to screw together the two halves.

"You buzz your lips against the mouthpiece," the student explained.

We all played instruments on and off for two years in this program. I soon found out my loaner trombone didn't work right. The two halves kept getting unscrewed and coming apart, prompting the trip to the music store with my dad.

Chapter 6
Creating Tone on a Cello

During the week following my first lesson with Mary Ann, I acquainted myself with the cello as best I could, which meant getting used to the awkwardness of holding the instrument correctly. It seemed so fragile. I was overly careful with it. Holding the bow took forever to get comfortable with. The weird grasp needed to hold the frog, while at the same time becoming accustomed to balancing the cello, was like doing the hula. A big problem arose when I adjusted the endpin to the right height. Instead of sticking to the floor, it slid out from underneath when practicing at home.

My hack to deal with this sent me to the garage. I dug around in my hiking gear, located a length of strong line, along with a carabiner and tied the line into a loop. A chair leg held one end. The endpin fit into the carabiner on the other end. To adjust the angle of the cello, I made the loop of the line longer or shorter.

Something else I soaked up while spending time with this rented cello was its tired, worn-out vibe. Since this was the only cello I'd ever played, and with nothing to compare it to, I had to go with my gut feeling rather than drawing on experience in playing a whole bunch of cellos. The rental couldn't have been that expensive to begin with, but what does a really good cello play like? How would I benefit from a better instrument?

I arrive early for everything, so I showed up twenty minutes before my next lesson to acclimate myself to the new surroundings. Lake Music has a music school feel about it, which I was becoming comfortable with, though most students are young.

Mary Ann sauntered in carrying a Subway sandwich and greeted me with "Hello, student. Let me open up my room and get the heater going—*brr*, it's always freezing in there." October in Oregon is when the weather starts to bottom out and turns gray and cool for months.

"I've been watching videos of Yo-Yo, studying the way he sits, but mostly the way he holds his fingers over the bow," I said proudly, as if I'd discovered some secret reservoir of knowledge only known to me. Who'd have thought of studying an internationally famous cellist to learn that?

"Yo-Yo's one of my favorite people, such a nice man. My stepson plays with him sometimes for his Silk Road project," Mary Ann said with a warm familiarity, as if they shared the special connection being professional musicians. "I've performed with him many times in the symphony. You'd like him."

"Really?" Mary Ann's involvement with one of the largest and oldest symphonies on the West Coast meant she'd played with practically everybody who was anybody in this end of the music spectrum.

"What's Yo-Yo like?" I asked.

"Great person. Really wonderful," Mary Ann said. "Remember, he's been playing and practicing for a long time. Let's get back to your lessons so you can catch up with him."

I adjusted my endpin, situated the cello both on and between my knees, but struggled to get my thumb happy in the little U-shaped notch in the frog. This particular bow had a squared-off corner at the end of that notch, jabbing my thumb and creating a sore spot. The whole bow thing, I just didn't get.

Our lesson began.

"I don't teach like other teachers. I start with tone. Creating a good tone is the foundation to playing the cello well. So, where do we begin?" she asked rhetorically. "Play a C."

I ran the bow over open C, causing a big old note to come out, which I thought sounded important and what a cello was supposed to sound like. C is the cello's lowest note.

"Try it again," she said. "Just press harder."

I repositioned the bow and pulled its entire length over the C string, which elongated the sound dramatically.

"Better. Play the note again, and this time, I'll add some pressure." She placed a finger on the tip of the bow and pressed down so the bow dragged heavily across the string.

"How did that sound? Better yet?" Mary Ann asked.

"I think so." I heard more muscle in the sound. More meat. Greater density.

"Now, same thing. I'm going to push down harder. And this time, pull the bow faster."

"Faster," I said.

The bow came across the string at three times the speed, vibrating the sound so I could feel it in my bones.

"Where'd that come from?" This is what the instrument is capable of, I realized.

"Speed and pressure create tone," Mary Ann proclaimed.

This second lesson moved pretty fast. Mary Ann was as calm as before. She complimented me for working at familiarizing myself with the instrument and the tricky bow. The music book she'd picked out for me was geared for adult beginners, skipping most of the elementary steps in learning to play. I could read music but was rusty. However, both the trombone and cello are C instruments with their music written in the bass clef. That familiarity ought to help me get started.

The last time I had blown a note out of a trombone was at the end of my freshman year in college—a lifetime ago. While I retained a familiarity with the bass clef, I barely remembered any of the names of the notes on the staff. Additionally, there are marks on cello sheet music to tell you to push or pull the bow. An arrow meant push. An open-bottom square meant pull. In an orchestra, these marks help the string players all move their bows in the same direction at the same time. It just cluttered the page to me, at least at this point.

I was exhausted at the end of the lesson. Thirty minutes can seem like an eternity when dealing with a crying child, investigating a leak from the ceiling in your bedroom, or being new to the cello. It is a physical instrument. It was fighting me, and there is a lot to keep under control. Each hand is doing something opposite from the other. Your arms move in different directions. Posture is important, but a struggle sitting upright, in my case from having blown out a disc in my lower back when playing too much volleyball years ago. The cello moves around when you play, tips side to side and swivels on the endpin. The mental challenge involved in coordinating all the moving parts while managing the bow and reading music is like juggling a watermelon, an apple, a pineapple and, let's say, a banana all at once.

"Why am I so determined to take on the cello at this point in my life? I don't understand what's driving me to do it," I said.

Mary Ann replied, "Why not? Its sound is beautiful. It has the range of a human voice, and you can sing every note it can play. Try it." I played the C string at the bottom of the cello's range. Sang that. Then worked my way up, singing the notes to prove the point. Mary Ann continued. "Right? The sound is comparable to someone singing. It makes perfect sense you want to play the cello."

As I left, Mary Ann walked me out to the store again, going over all the new things I'd learned that day. "Look at all the things you know how to do now that you didn't know when you came in here today." She ticked off details about holding the bow, playing "Twinkle" one more time, exploring the promise of speed and pressure producing a rich tone.

As the weekly lessons went along, we worked foremost on getting a consistent, rich tone. You hear about all the scratching sounds string players make when learning how their instrument works. These sounds usually come from moving the bow too slowly and not pushing down hard enough on the strings.

"Speed and pressure create tone. Can you hear it?" Mary Ann asked during another lesson. "Try it again."

I pulled the bow over a string faster, pressing down hard. "It's a richer sound," I answered even though I had little to compare it to. I spent a little time each day discovering how to get the instrument lined up with my knees in place. Adjusting the endpin, finding the best tilt for the cello as the instrument lay back on my sternum. Getting the bow situated with the dodgy grasp of the frog.

"Try it four more times. Pepperoni pizza on each string," she said.

Mary Ann showed me a card with a lot of squares. In each square was a cartoon with a word broken into syllables, creating a rhythm to play to. The syllables express the rhythm. "Pep-per-o-ni-pi-zza" created a rhythm of four short beats and two long beats.

The cartoon piece of pizza sat in the square with these words on it. I played the rhythm, following the pattern, while adding pressure and speed to enrich the tone. This technique also helped me understand how to play the cello louder.

"It's surprising how much volume you can get out of this." I patted the front.

"There's more in there, trust me. Play loud, you can always reduce the volume. Don't be afraid to play loud," she said.

I began noticing things and asking a few of the right questions. What an accomplishment to reach just that level. In an effort to sound encouraging, she went on to tell me about other students who have far more trouble and don't figure these things out.

"Some students don't ask many questions. They follow instructions, but when they make a mistake, they don't work to figure out the reason. If they did that, it would help them learn faster," she said.

Mary Ann's knack for generously giving compliments did a lot to encourage me. We went over fingering after that, finding how notes follow one another up and down a scale and how they're not evenly spaced.

"You have the advantage of reading music," she mentioned several times. "A lot of people can't do that, so they're learning all that at the same time they work out where the notes are on the fingerboard. It's like learning a couple new languages at the same time. Along with juggling everything else that's happening."

Amazing how much I wanted to become competent at this. The coordination required proved complicated. My left hand began to find the invisible spots on the fingerboard you pressed to hit the right note, then lost them. My right hand and arm operated the bow, which doesn't just saw back and forth; it moves in every direction, but needs to be controlled. I began to manage the main body of the cello more easily as I learned how it wanted to bob around the way a dingy rights itself in a summer gale. Finding the correct tilt without letting the endpin slide out from under the instrument and clunking myself in the head with the tuning pegs next to my ear was a wrestling match.

"Let's see if we're in tune," Mary Ann said. "Let's review. The strings are tuned in fifths, right? C, G, D, and A. Cellos always go flat because of the weather."

"The tuning pegs slip," I added.

"Yes, especially this time of year."

Two days after having been warned of the changing weather, I found the C string on my cello unraveled, looking like an uncoiled spring. The tuning peg came loose enough to fall out, looking as if someone had deliberately untightened it. The cello was obviously alive and reacting to its environment.

I didn't want to break the thing by trying to repair it. When I pinged her, Mary Ann told me to take my rental to Tim at the music store. He put rosin all over the loose peg, then stuck the peg back in and tightened it up. You can do that on a tired, old rental instrument, but not with a higher quality cello, as I assumed it wouldn't need it.

Which got me to thinking: I hadn't paid a lot of attention to how much these lessons cost. They seemed quite reasonable and included the rental instrument. When I asked Tim, he told me I was accumulating a down payment to buy a cello. There'd been no discussion about this, nothing about saving to buy a cello at his shop. If I bought one, I assumed I would go to a shop that specialized in high-quality string instruments rather than the student-level cellos they had at Lake Music.

I needed to think about what to do about this, so I started by cancelling the saving plan and just paying for lessons.

Chapter 7
Perfumed Spit Towels

In junior high—they weren't calling them middle schools yet—our band director was a gentleman with high-top dress shoes and a polite manner named Carlyle Hume. He would often say, "I'm from Missouri, show me," if we made an excuse about something. I stuck with playing trombone when I moved up to junior high and, for the first time, played in a band with all the different instruments together.

Mr. Hume played the trumpet. We'd hear him practicing between classes and during his preparation hour. When we were playing in class, and he thought we were making a musical blunder, he would walk to his office and return with his trumpet to perform for us. Everybody liked him. He clearly enjoyed teaching music and was always in good humor.

One result of blowing a horn—trumpet, trombone, tuba—is it fills with saliva. The trombone has a spit valve at the bottom of the slide. When the instrument fills with an ocean of slobber, you press the valve, and it all drains out. Tuba players turn the instrument upside down to drain the bell. Mr. Hume's band room was littered with towels all over the floor to empty spit onto. These towels were always damp, which I didn't pay much attention to until it dawned on me why they were damp.

"Can I take these towels home and wash them?" I asked my band director.

Mr. Hume gave me a puzzled look. "Sure, why don't you do that."

My parents greeted the arrival of large bags of spit towels with a disengaged wariness. "They came from where?" my father asked.

When we ran the towels through the washer and dryer, they magically became white and bright. Mr. Hume's spit towels were new again. If that didn't demonstrate my enthusiastic support of the school music program, what would? Better than that, I thought about how I might improve these towels. Wouldn't they be more refreshing and stay usable longer if they carried a refreshing scent? Could I perfume them?

The answer to this question, of course, was no, don't do that. However, I was all of thirteen years old at the time, so I would let nothing interfere with my bad judgment.

For weeks the band room smacked of the cut-rate *eau de toilette* from the bottle I'd found at the back of my parents' bathroom cabinet. Still, Mr. Hume remained appreciative of the towels being washed. Though he commented a few times on "that horrible aroma" and told us he'd take care of the towels from then on.

The experience with Mr. Hume kept me interested in the band program as he was so nice and easy to work with. However, I was to learn that high school band was a whole different animal. I looked forward to the marching band. Trombone players stand in the first row because of the slides, which require plenty of space in front to keep from stabbing anyone who might be marching in front of them.

At Crawford High School, our band director, Mr. Robinette, gave us a big change from easygoing, mellow Mr. Hume. Robinette had to deal with full-blown teenagers in their last years of compulsory education. There were a lot of factors adding to the strain. With more than five thousand students, Crawford was one of the largest high schools in California and remained over-stuffed with way too many students for years, as the San Diego Public Schools took their sweet time getting around to building a new high school.

The most arresting feature of my new band room was an enormous chart mounted above the chalkboard titled "Dings" in big letters. Every time a band member misbehaved, they received a ding. Too many dings meant some sort of punishment got doled out. Dings primarily went to the boys who couldn't sit still and had energy to burn off. Having a huge chart on the wall with your name on it was meant to dissuade you from misbehaving rather than creating a competition to see who could chalk up the most.

Mr. Robinette knew there weren't many good high school musicians to begin with. He'd been a high school band director long enough to understand how a band worked. When a trumpet player came along who had a knack for the instrument, could play good and loud with good tone, their bad behavior was largely ignored.

I liked Mr. Robinette. While he wasn't a Mr. Hume, I sensed Robinette understood the pressures of being a teenager. When he came down on one of us too hard, he famously apologized later one on one. This made a big difference when he called me out a couple times. I felt devoted to band and the program, and I made a lot of friends there.

Everyone knew our current drum major, Joyce, would graduate, and I had my eye on replacing her. My dad had been the drum major at San Diego High School during the 1920s. He became a musician when his parents bought him a drum set because he banged on all the pots and pans and they couldn't get him to stop.

He also played a little in vaudeville, performing once in an orchestra for a show with Eddie Cantor, who was a big star at the time. There was a bit Dad was supposed to help with that involved tearing some fabric when Cantor bent over to simulate his pants being ripped. There was no rehearsal, Dad missed the cue, and Cantor chewed him out after the show.

There are photos of him playing with the San Diego Symphony and with his own band, The Five Aces. He played the summer season at Yellowstone National Park in the Old Faithful Lodge ballroom. Back then there was a live band and dancing every night.

He spent his entire adult life searching for the photo taken of him in his drum major uniform, leading the band with John Philip Sousa, the great composer and conductor, watching from in front of the landmark US Grant Hotel. It would have been taken around 1927. If you happen to find it, I'd like a copy.

He always kept his drum set in the living room but never let me touch it. Never taught me a thing about the drums.

Toward the end of the year, I approached Mr. Robinette at the right moment and told him, "I'd like to be drum major next year."

He seemed to tuck that away.

What seemed like an eternity later, the band members and parents gathered for a year-end ceremony in the school cafeteria. Toward the end of the event, I was at the front with some other students, and Mr. Robinette turned off the microphone and leaned over to me.

"Can I announce you'll be drum major next year?" he asked quietly.

"Yes," I said.

I thought he'd forgotten.

Mr. Robinette turned the microphone back on and announced "And George will be our new drum major next year."

The evening ended with Robinette saying he'd taken a job with a different school in the county, which was known to have stronger, better-funded band programs. A man named Dennis would be next year's band director. We knew nothing about him.

Chapter 8
Good Teacher, Bad Teacher

In the hottest part of that summer, my parents drove me to the University of Redlands in the desert east of San Bernardino, near Palm Springs. They checked me in at drum major camp and headed on to Las Vegas, promising to pick me up on the way back at the end of the week.

A summer camp for high school drum majors had been operating on the Redlands campus for years. A great many of us from Southern California attended to familiarize ourselves with marching in formation, handling batons, blowing whistle commands, steering the band, and marching around corners—all that and more.

We stayed in the dorms, ate in the cafeteria, and marched in the parking lot under the desert sun. I shared a room with the drum major from Tustin High School. Our concrete dorm had a large basement with a metal fallout shelter sign attached to the wall over the entrance. In a moment of weakness, I pried it off the wall and kept the sign in my bedroom for years—leaving me forever concerned that, in case of nuclear attack, no one on that campus would know where to hide.

I don't remember the name of the man who ran the camp, but calling him Ralph works. What he did for a living the rest of the year wasn't clear, but he had a great time running the program. He explained his qualifications to us, repeating them daily throughout the week. Ralph had to be fifty or so.

"I am a champion baton twirler," Ralph began and went on about the baton performance awards he'd won. "I've roller-skated in the Pasadena Tournament of Roses Parade, twirling my baton twenty-three years in a row," Ralph proclaimed. He talked about other contests of different kinds where he'd wear a colorful costume—silky with sparkles sewn by his mother or perhaps a costumer in the motion-picture business.

About halfway through the week, we tired of hearing this, and the next time he mentioned roller skating and baton twirling in the Rose Parade, one of the girls from a far corner of LA chanted, "Roller skate. Roller skate. Roller skate." Many joined in.

The temperature by noon in Redlands hit 102 or higher every day. They were scorchers. Visualize a marching band of drum majors carrying batons, practicing their skills by marching back and forth in formation under a desert sun. Every day someone had to drop out and find shade to avoid a trip to the emergency department for sunstroke.

A highlight of the week involved a dinner in the cafeteria. A cafeteria worker accidently lost control of a cart, dumping fifty gallons of red fruit punch in a waterfall on her head. Otherwise, we were hot, tired, and thirsty and too exhausted to laugh at anything.

By the time my parents picked me up on their way back from Vegas, I knew enough basics to lead a band, blow commands on a whistle, wheel the oversized drum major's baton in the air, and turn a band around a corner during a parade.

A few weeks later, my junior year at Will C. Crawford began, and the band would adjust to the new teacher, Dennis Foster.

Dennis seemed unsure of himself from the minute we entered the band room. We sensed his lack of ease and talked about it among ourselves. We learned that we were his first major teaching assignment at a large high school with an active band program. He wasn't even thirty years old yet, not that much older than we were. Dennis also seemed to see everyone as a discipline problem, as he wasn't used to channeling our teenage energy effectively.

That I couldn't sit still and got bored fast didn't help. Having the responsibilities of being drum major for the upcoming football season as well as in a parade here and there, I looked forward to the fantastic experience of leading a marching band. Having a compassionate mentor to help me navigate would have been a great help, but Dennis just didn't have the capacity to offer this.

"Did you go to drum major camp?" was the first thing Dennis asked when he saw me.

"Yes, at Redlands. I was there for a week," I said. He didn't ask for more than that. At no point did he take time to have a conversation with me about his expectations, how he wanted me to conduct myself, or what I was to do. He never initiated a discussion about what a leadership role would look like with him as the new band director. Dennis didn't share his experience in marching bands either, though he had certainly participated in them.

During rehearsals, I played the trombone, bad as I was. I kept playing in the brass section of the orchestra, pep band too. We played at basketball games and even pep rallies during lunch to rev up student excitement for Friday night football games.

In the spring, Dennis decided he wanted to organize a stage band, a dance band like those on late-night TV talk shows. This was a personal interest he had, and it seemed like his hobby.

Dennis recruited players, including me, for this. He wanted us to come in an hour before classes started to rehearse. This involved my figuring out an earlier ride to school, getting an hour less sleep, and cutting into what little free time I had. I went along with this to be cooperative without thinking about the time involved. We didn't get any extra credit, no performances were scheduled, plus it involved another rehearsal on top of everything else going on.

But I was consumed by band, showed up, and played my trombone in this group too.

After a few months, Dennis' shoulders dropped when I told him I couldn't manage adding another musical commitment to everything else I was involved with. It was just too much. He acted like I'd stabbed him in the back.

The music program became to me, and many others, all about disliking how Dennis ran the program but making the best of it. He didn't have the skills to develop a positive rapport, at least not this early into his teaching career. Dennis started to drive me away from music.

At the same time, I got help on my drum majoring from Terry O'Donnell, who won great admiration as the drum major at San Diego State. Thin and compact, he cut an energetic figure in his uniform with a tall shako hat and energetic routine.

Everybody in the Southern California band scene knew Terry. He seemed to appear at every musical event anywhere and developed a helpful, positive reputation in the music community. On the field leading a college halftime show, he had ways to twirl the drum major baton smoothly, throw it in the air, and catch it to project energy into a sold-out football stadium.

As an accomplished drum major, his signature move was The Run. He would stand at attention at the back of the band as it stood in formation on the football field. A big drum roll would build to a peak as Terry ran through the middle of the musicians. But this wasn't any old run. As he hurled himself forward, he tipped back, appearing to lean parallel to the ground, legs kicking out in front of him, white shoes and spats in the air.

This drew thunderous applause, becoming his signature move at many halftime shows, igniting the crowd before the team ran onto the field.

Terry taught me to do The Run and some trick baton-twirling moves, along with a way to toss the baton over my head and catch it. This was amazingly wonderful, especially in contrast to my own band director who kept an impersonal distance and only voiced complaints. Terry went on to study conducting, winding up as a music professor and, after that, a musical theater director for years. He still plays piano in musicals and remains a fixture in San Diego music circles.

When I told Dennis about special drum major lessons, I expected him to be delighted. Why wouldn't he want the best high school drum major possible? Instead, he showed faint interest and in no way acknowledged taking additional training as an indication of my devotion to our music program. Nevertheless, I persisted. I told him about being able to do The Run, asking if the move could be added to the upcoming halftime show. "I'll think about it," he mumbled, and I waited. At the last minute before one halftime show, he agreed to the addition. I pulled off the run perfectly—or at least as best I could.

Everything, so far as I was concerned, went well enough my first year as drum major in the Crawford High School band. I spent all my time thinking music program, band, orchestra. When I walked around campus, I thought about my posture, how many steps I took so they were measured, stepping off on a walk with my left foot as bands do. Still, Dennis wanted perfect behavior from his students and evidently did not remember challenges of being a teenager or understand the additional issues of the time.

Another big musical event on the horizon was the talent show, which would be performed during lunchtime. The auditorium would be packed. Our school had so many students, there were three starting times for students in the morning and three lunch breaks, which meant performing three shows.

I recruited a few fellow musicians to form a band to perform at this show. We called ourselves the New Salvation Posi-Traction Tug Boat Band. A hit song at the time called "Winchester Cathedral" came from one of the British Invasion groups, the New Vaudeville Band. It was a campy number with lyrics like, "Oh-vo-de-oh-doe" in Rudy Vallée style.

The Tug Boats played three tunes for a packed auditorium. I banged on the tambourine and sang through a little megaphone to great applause. Dennis attended but never acknowledged our performance or recognized my initiative in pulling The Tug Boat Band together. If Dennis couldn't be the man in front waving his arms at the young musicians, he couldn't be bothered. But we were making music, creating a band with liveliness, generating spontaneous enthusiasm at a school assembly.

Report cards at the time were done by hand on a triplicate form. We carried them from class to class on report card day. Halfway through the first semester of my senior year, I got the automatic A everyone expected from band. This grade didn't count officially but was meant to give you guidance about how you were doing for the term. And didn't everybody in band get an A?

However, at the end of the fall semester, for the permanent grade marked on my report card, Dennis gave me a B. He'd clearly decided he didn't like me, and this was how he would put me in my place. I'm sure I sounded and acted like a seventeen-year-old, but a B in band? With all the work I put in? All the hours? Extra performances with the orchestra and everything else?

Nobody gets a B in band.

I went up to him at the end of class.

"You accidently gave me a B," I said, expecting him to recognize and correct his mistake.

"No, that's your grade." Dennis shuffled his feet a bit, as if caught doing something he thought he'd silently get away with. Other students were listening nearby. He had expected no pushback.

"I don't understand," I said. "This is on my permanent record. On the last report card, you gave me an A."

"You did better in the first half. You didn't do as well in the second half." He clearly did not expect me to bring this up to him, or that he'd have to defend himself. Especially directly to me in front of a bunch of other students who were standing around listening.

"I don't believe this is right. I would have had to earn a C this second half of the semester to average down to a B," I reasoned.

This may sound small and unimportant, but it mattered in a big way. In a music program, you establish a lot of camaraderie with other kids, make a lot of friends. Plus, everybody knew me because I played in so many groups and was the drum major. The reason Dennis did this was incomprehensible, amounting to an enormous betrayal by a teacher.

"I'm not going to change your grade," Dennis said twice when I continued to ask him to explain whatever logic he used to give me a B. What had I done? It seemed he just wanted to project a sense of authority without knowing how to go about it.

That evening, I shared how despondent I felt with my parents, how unfair this was, insisting they do something. Being school teachers themselves, I figured they'd see my side, but they were hesitant to do anything. As usual, it was impossible to get my mother's attention. She gave her opinion about everything freely so long as it had something to do with her but never showed any willingness to help anyone else. Her contribution to my musical experience growing up didn't rise above morose, plodding renditions of dreary tunes on our piano as she descended into woe. Gloominess was her original factory setting.

Dad finally called the school and talked with Dennis, who insisted he wouldn't change my grade, but still couldn't provide a reason for the B other than the nonspecific, "He didn't do as well the second half of the semester." Totally bunk.

My dad didn't have much nerve when it came to standing up for things. He complained a lot in private but didn't have the gumption to follow through when it came to the crunch. He never figured out how to be much of an advocate for me in the best of times, so I'm not so sure he made much of an effort.

Nonetheless, he did express disdain for Dennis doing this, being a former drum major himself and having taught in both high school and college. "They don't have any test to grade you, so how can he mark you down?" Dad said far more insistently to me in our living room than I'm sure he sounded on the phone to Dennis. "He's playing favorites!" he said to me, though I doubt he'd have the brass to say it to my music teacher.

The next day I went straight to Dennis again without paying any notice to the dozen students herding around me to listen to the exchange. In high school I felt I could do this. Again, I asked for an explanation, only to get the same old "You did better in the first half of the semester" from him.

I went on to tell him what my dad said: "You're playing favorites. This is wrong, and I deserve an A like everybody else."

Clearly, clearly, clearly, this teacher—this new music teacher—realized he'd made a mistake. Dennis looked quietly horrified that every last student in the band knew what he'd done and that he never provided an explanation. He just would not admit his mistake.

Was this what creating music was really about? What happened to the simple joy that brought me to it?

I headed for the counseling office and asked for a different class. Something else. Not music. What could I move into if I was going to be treated like this? They told me I could graduate without band. Still, my high school activities revolved around the music program. That's where my friends were. I'd been betrayed. But since there was only half a school year left until I graduated, there wasn't an easy alternative class to move me into.

I dropped out of all music activities except what I had to do to play third trombone in band. I didn't exchange a word with Dennis the rest of the year. He gave me an automatic A for my final semester. I even led the band one more time in a parade in the spring. But I never felt the same about music.

Decades later, mention of Dennis popped up on an alumni website. He'd retired to Arizona after being a high school band director a long time. The website provided his email address, so I sent him a message to verify he was the same Dennis Foster who I'd worked with, and not someone with the same name. He replied right away, as though I were a favorite student from his first-year teaching, when he was just learning to run a high school music program. He sounded chatty, and his message had the tone of wanting to relive some nonexistent good old days. He wrote about his career, where he taught, and his retirement.

Once I knew for sure I was corresponding with my Dennis, I sent him a message from my point of view after decades of perspective.

First, I reminded him of the substandard grade he gave me without any explanation—the B. Then I carefully explained that I felt his marking me down without any explanation came from his inexperience and immaturity as a new teacher.

"Every little flute player who never did anything except show up the minimum amount of time in class got an A. I was the only student in the program you gave a B." Then I explained that I experienced his action as a betrayal of a student who trusted him and that I couldn't trust a teacher again after that—which is true. His actions redefined my view of teachers.

Most importantly, I asked him this question: "Why didn't you take the opportunity to have conversations with me, give guidance and advice? I could have remembered you as a great mentor. You could have taken the opportunity to talk with me, set expectations, explain what you were looking for in the responsibilities I was given."

I wrote in my message, "You obviously realized you'd made a mistake, everyone could see that. But you didn't have the maturity to admit the error and fix it."

I never received a response from Dennis. Not one peep. His lack of leadership forever changed how I felt about music. My first year in college I played trombone in the marching band. We performed halftime shows in a packed football stadium. Even played in the stands for a football game in the Pasadena Rose Bowl.

That was enough formal music education for me. I put my trombone away for good at the end of that semester. Years later, I donated the trombone to the city schools so other students could give it a try.

When searching for a music teacher, find yourself a Mary Ann Coggins Kaza. Stay clear of a Dennis Foster.

More than half a century after I graduated from high school and received that B from Dennis, I still see some of the kids who I was in band with back then. We're old now, but still meet at reunions, plus some of us continue to stay in touch otherwise. When I asked them if I should write about this part of our shared musical experience in my story about learning the cello, they encouraged me to include it. They insisted I be honest and talk about what it was like then and how we experienced this teacher's conduct toward us. How it changed my relationship with music.

Along these lines, I recently met the writer Anne Lamott when taking a workshop at her house and spoke with her in the kitchen. We stood along a wall with boxes of breakfast cereal and jars of jam. I told her, "I thought I'd meet you someday, though I didn't think it would be in your kitchen."

She graciously called me "young man," though I was probably the oldest person attending. We talked a little about honesty in writing and its importance, especially when you are older and don't have the time or desire to skirt the truth. She encourages writers to tell the truth, and I have done that here.

Anne Lamott said in her bestseller about writing, *Bird by Bird*: "You own everything that happened to you. Tell your stories. If people wanted you to write warmly about them, they should have behaved better."

This story about Dennis Foster belongs to me. It is part of my musical journey. He was a lousy music teacher and should have behaved better. Don't let your music teacher pull a Dennis on you.

Chapter 9
Show Biz and Carpet in the Bathroom

I'd given up musical instruments, I thought, but wound up auditioning for musicals once I became a theater major in college. To my joy, I was cast in the classic show *Guys and Dolls*. The part was Arvide Abernathy, a bass drum–toting Salvation Army granddad who sings the sentimental song, "More I Cannot Wish You," in an Irish accent. I hadn't done any acting, nothing like a big main stage musical with a bunch of other students, and wondered if I could pull it off.

I worked at an Irish accent, played the part, and sang the song. Getting cast in a college production—especially a musical—was hard because the audition draws non-majors who try out for nothing else and want a shot at singing and dancing on stage. Hundreds try out. I auditioned again the next year but didn't get a part in *Fiddler on the Roof*.

However, the next summer, nearby Grossmont Community College posted auditions for another musical, *Cabaret*. Since I was a couple years older than most of these students, I thought I had a shot at the lead role playing the American living in Berlin, Clifford Bradshaw.

After a quick audition process, I got that part too, amazingly. The role proved to be the height of my musical theater career. The community college operation ran on a tight budget, underfunded like most arts programs, so it took a lot of improvisation and scrounging by the staff to bring a production to life. The counterweight system in the small theater used a variety of locally gathered rocks to fly the scenery. The sets were modest but inventive, built by the teacher who directed the show. He also had a dance scene with the master of ceremonies in which he wore a gorilla costume.

The show was fun and didn't have any of the patina of main stage importance of the larger state college stage. A live student orchestra played the music. They were situated in front of the raised stage apron between the actors and the audience. During one of the performances, the conductor, a music professor, screwed up a cue for a song in the scene before I went on. He became so discombobulated by his error that he totally missed my next song all together.

I plowed ahead, and without the orchestra starting up, I had to sing it a cappella. An expression of horror grew on the conductor's face as I completed the entire song unaccompanied. The show was so informal that the audience and cast even met in the hallway at intermission to chat about how it was going.

I took two singing lessons from the music professor after the show was finished. We did these in his living room, while he played his piano. I wish I'd been able to take advantage of his teaching skills before I'd sung in any musicals.

"Send the sound up through the top of your head. Stand up straight. Open your mouth and let the sound vibrate your teeth." He raised his hand toward the ceiling to show me how to project a note.

This advice proved helpful, even in public speaking when wanting to—musically—have my voice heard in a theater. If I ever found myself onstage in a theater again, I would utilize those lessons.

A couple of my fellow theater students at San Diego State went on to professional careers, most prominently Julie Kavner, who created the voice of Marge Simpson on the long-running show, *The Simpsons*. Julie was cast in a lot of shows, and we were in several classes together. She is one of the nicest, brightest people I've ever met. I'm proud of her success, the way fellow students can be for one another.

Another student I worked with in a college TV production was Carl Weathers. He sang a song when I was the floor manager for a student show. Weathers played football briefly, then went on to Hollywood where he acted in movies and television shows, notably playing Apollo Creed in the *Rocky* movies.

The summer after college graduation, I had another brush with professional music performance, where I learned what really goes on backstage. The campus had an old outdoor theater used for a variety of events. The layout suggested the ancient Greek design, basically half a circle with concrete seats ascending the side of a hill. The stage area backed up to the campus library, creating something close enough to a classic setting for performing Greek-style scenes during acting classes outdoors.

I was hired as the theater's backstage manager, handling the university's side of the summer season for the San Diego Symphony and Starlight Opera Company, a liaison between the school and professional groups.

The symphony scheduled guest artists, pianists, dancers, and conductors. Starlight Opera was a community theater running outdoor summer musicals. For years, these ran in an outdoor theater under the flight path of landing airplanes at the San Diego airport, which is irrationally located downtown. The noise grew so immense as planes got larger that the theater became unusable and fled inland to the Greek Bowl.

That summer's shows were *The Music Man,* starring Charles Nelson Reilly, and *Show Boat.* Charles Nelson Reilly was a comedic actor with Broadway and Hollywood credentials. He put on a snide, dry, snake-like persona. His relationship with the rest of the cast of local amateur actors was distant, confounded by the fact that he didn't know his lines. His performance left the audience wondering if he would remember the next thing to say or make it to the end of the show.

When he forgot a line during rehearsals, he'd stop the show and blame the orchestra for distracting him.

"Too much talking in the pit! I can't work this way," Reilly yelled to stop the rehearsal when he didn't know his line. He never had his heart in the show. It seemed like he only wanted to hurry back to Beverly Hills rather than throw himself into creating a quality production.

Charles Nelson Reilly was a good reality check about the musical theater business for me. I was surprised by how little effort a professional at Reilly's level would put into a fun gig. In TV interviews later, he admitted, "I did *Music Man* in San Diego and blew it." No, what really happened, Mr. Reilly, was you didn't put any effort into it and phoned in your performance.

The musical, *Show Boat,* had the same live orchestra and a local cast that summer, but without a blustery star. This made it a greater success and much easier to watch.

The symphony performances I helped manage that summer included several musical guest stars. I met them all, watching them demonstrate the professional side of the music they played. Country music star Chet Atkins was a smooth, folksy, inventive guitar player and record company executive. In my position, I had a chance to talk with Chet and his crew backstage. He was polite and quiet, easy to work with. When he fumbled playing a riff during the show, he simply said, "Oh, Lordy," and kept going.

I still remember a joke he told with a country-boy innocence. During a pause in his playing, Chet looked over his guitar at the audience.

"We finally got around putting carpet in the bathroom," he said, strumming his guitar. "One of these days we're going to run it all the way into the house."

The other visiting luminary I interacted with at length was Arthur Fiedler, long-time conductor of the Boston Pops. Fiedler was internationally famous for bringing concerts to the masses, making them easy to listen to and enjoy. He so endeared himself to Boston that a truck-size abstract statue of his head, with flowing hair and walrus mustache, stands along the Charles River Esplanade.

Fiedler played the violin, piano, organ, and percussion, working his way up the musical ladder to become the conductor of the Boston Pops Orchestra in 1930. The Pops made music accessible by shortening the program and playing crowd-pleasers, such as "A Turkey in the Straw." When he conducted this particularly lively number, he encouraged people to clap along, then turned to the audience and cut them off with a wave of his baton—great fun.

My experience with Maestro Fiedler helped me understand what can happen under the pressures of being famous in the music business. He arrived for a few days of rehearsals and concerts with the San Diego Symphony as a renowned conductor with broad audience appeal. Fiedler stood out in a crowd with his long, swept-back white hair and walrus moustache recognizable at great distance. At the time, he was a titanic musical icon. I showed him the backstage spaces, his dressing room, access to the stage. Two assistants accompanied him when he first arrived.

As the days progressed, he showed up at the theater early for rehearsals and performances with a member of the symphony staff. One evening, as he walked along the backstage pathway toward me, I realized something alarming. I had never before seen anyone so completely drunk and still able to stand on two feet. It was as shocking as seeing something as recognizable as, say, the Statue of Liberty teetering and tipping, shuffling along the path.

"Where the hell is my restroom?" Arthur Fiedler snarled.

"Right through that door," I said, pointing toward where he had to go, but he started walking the wrong way, toward the audience seating.

"The audience's restrooms are in that direction," I said.

He made a slow turn to look me in the eye. "I don't care about the audience's restrooms. Where is mine?" He mumbled, "Send me in the wrong direction. Who's in charge here?"

Again, I indicated the direction he was supposed to go, hoping he wouldn't get lost so fast this time. Fiedler would, after all, soon be in charge of a full-blown symphony orchestra in front of a packed house—thousands of people watching.

"This is an abomination," Fiedler sputtered, tilting on his feet.

Rather than try further navigation, he took matters into his own hands. The world-famous Boston Pops conductor wandered over to a wall along the path leading to the dressing room and answered nature's call in the bushes for what seemed like half an hour.

What more was there to learn about the world of music professionals?

After that, I moved to Minnesota for grad school and stayed for a long time. There, my relationship to music—at least organized instrument playing, practicing, and enjoying it—didn't take any particular shape. When rock star Kenny Loggins came to town, I learned an old high school friend worked on his touring crew. Mark Wittenberg was the roadie who wrangled Kenny's guitars. He tuned them offstage, then handed off one guitar for another during the show. When strings broke, Mark replaced them.

He got me those special tickets roadies get for friends, seats at the apron of the stage, in front of the most expensive seats. Studying rock-and-roll musicians strutting their stuff that close during a live show in a sold-out auditorium for free helped me understand all the hours they put into it and what is expected of them.

Great experience. I've seen Queen, Wings, the Rolling Stones, and the Beach Boys live several times. I feel a connection with the Beach Boys because we grew up at the same time in the same corner of the country when they were on the rise in Southern California.

While in Minnesota, I took a run at learning piano with Jimmy Hamilton, a Black musician with great improvisational skills. He played with Ray Charles' band. Also told me he was Prince's high school band teacher.

"Prince could play any instrument," Hamilton recalled. "I needed a sousaphone player. Didn't have one. I told Prince I'd give him ten dollars if he'd play sousaphone for me. He went right out and did it. Figured out the valve fingering on his own, just like that."

Jimmy Hamilton did his best to introduce me to improvisation on the piano by reading charts, which is basic sheet music melody line with the chords noted. I enjoyed this experience immensely and showed up whenever he was performing to study the way he played. Still, I simply didn't connect with the piano as closely or as quickly as I would with the cello.

The piano doesn't require as much work to get a rich, clear tone the way the cello does. You just hit a key, and the note comes out. Maybe I looked at the piano as a piece of furniture I visited to play and didn't feel I could become a part of it the same way.

Chapter 10
Violin in the Attic

Mary Ann took up the violin in fourth grade when the students in her class were told to bring an instrument to school to form a band. She rummaged around the house looking for an instrument and wound up in the attic, where she found a violin. She didn't mention she wanted to try it out since she thought it was her sister's, who might have told her she couldn't use it.

Playing the violin hadn't been mentioned before by her family. There are undoubtedly a million violins in attics and basements and closets, long forgotten after a grandparent or someone in the family took a run at it. Mary Ann said that once she discovered the violin in the attic, she snuck the instrument to school.

During music class, she received some instruction about how to play. She kept her interest in the violin a secret by hiding the instrument in the bushes in front of her house when she got home.

"When my parents came to school for a show, they were surprised to see me playing the violin in the band. They couldn't believe it," Mary Ann said. "My teacher was a bass player with the Portland Symphony. He was an artiste who wore purple pants and a green jacket. He told my parents I had a knack for playing violin, and he was willing to give me free lessons if they agreed."

Her father replied, "I will pay for her lessons."

From there, Mary Ann kept learning the violin. "The inspiration to improve increases the more you learn and play," she told me.

Young students usually play a fractionally sized instrument when they're young. There are one-eighth–size violins and cellos for growing kids, leading up to full-size instruments, so as students grow, they can move up to a larger size. Mary Ann always played full-size violins.

"Finding the violin was an opportunity, which led to a career," Mary Ann said. "It taught me not to pass up an opportunity when it comes along.

"Another opportunity started me teaching. I buy violin strings at Lake Music because I like to shop in my neighborhood. I could buy these cheaper online, but who does that help out? I came in one day just at the right moment to start teaching here," Mary Ann said.

"Have you always taught students in addition to playing professionally?" I asked.

"Some, but I've taught a lot more since I came in here and wound up talking to Tim, the owner. He said his strings teacher had just quit, and he needed a violin and cello teacher. Maybe someone to teach some piano and bass too," she said. "Tim hired me for my experience. Other places would prefer to hire twenty-year-olds rather than older people. They want vacant minds rather than older, experienced minds. At seventy-seven, trust me, my mind's experienced. Five years after I started here, I have a steady stream of students."

On a recent Thursday, when she arrived at Lake Music to teach, a staff member handed her a list of students for the day. This list changed constantly due to new students, make-up lessons, people out of town, and other adjustments.

"I start with you at one and will go straight through with thirty-minute lessons until after eight o'clock," she told me. "I do this three days a week."

"Do you teach school kids mostly?"

"Everybody. Lots of young people. Adults like you. Some people played in high school and want to take it up again later. Adults often have a preconceived notion of an instrument, so that requires a different approach to realign them with the reality of playing."

One of her students hid the fact they'd played for eleven years when young and were restarting all these years later. They didn't want to be embarrassed they hadn't retained anything from their youth.

Mary Ann went on. "Some parents treat music lessons as babysitting. They want to drop off the kid and pick them up later. I make them stay and either sit in the hallway or in the room during the lesson. Parents need to support their young musicians. Parents who couldn't care less have apathy, which is our enemy. Music solves a lot of problems. Countries that lose their ability to have orchestras are in decline."

She explained how students at Lake Music don't necessarily want to become musicians or even professional musicians. "They just want to understand more about music, so taking on an instrument becomes another part of their experience. Students need to experiment. Repetition is our friend," she said. "I work to keep students going, keep them interested. I don't have them do scales. Scales are the old, traditional, disciplined way to teach. They're boring, and students hate them."

Mary Ann gave me a music sheet with scales, but we talked nothing more about scales, other than mentioning they help to learn to play in different keys. I felt grateful for not having to endure the monotony of scales.

"Read a note, make a sound, play a tune," she said.

She works to win over students, especially young students, because this involves winning over the parent too. "Once they understand you're being honest, they attach to you for life. Students become a part of your big musical family. Also, I tell students to play with the lights off, or their eyes closed, so they don't look when they play. It helps with muscle memory."

Chapter 11
The Cello Bank

During my first three lessons using the rented student cello, I picked up hints from Mary Ann that there were better cellos out there. She seldom came straight out and said things. Instead, she gave examples, letting me draw my own conclusions.

"The better the cello, the easier it is to play," she said.

Additionally, whenever she talked about tone—which was all the time—she'd say getting the robust sound I wanted isn't always easy from an inexpensive factory instrument, such as the one I was playing.

I fled to the internet again, broadening my search for a cello, probably not the most reliable place to find trustworthy information, but a start. Searched the Craigslist ads first and found the people offering their instruments for sale didn't include many details, even where their cello was made. Perhaps they didn't know. Maybe they didn't pay that much attention, or it didn't matter when buying the inexpensive instrument collecting dust bunnies around it in a closet. Most of the cellos listed for sale were beginner models rather than quality instruments with a pedigree. Some were half or quarter size for kids, but they didn't always post that information accurately.

What was a reliable, trustworthy source when hunting for a good, affordable cello? I continued searching "cellos for sale near me," bringing up a thunderous mountain of these creatures for sale, some from hundreds of miles away. In a few pictures, the listed cellos looked beat up, as if they'd been thrown down a flight of stairs. Some appeared way too perfect, the owners taking care to photograph them in their living rooms with favorable lighting or with a roaring fireplace in the background. A few looked like they were made of a material akin to cardboard rather than wood.

I found the prices for these used instruments set ultra-low, as if they could be used for spare parts, the way someone owning an old car that doesn't run might part it out. It would be plainly impossible that used cellos of this ilk could be expected to produce the kind of tone and easy playability Mary Ann had in mind.

Cellos posted for sale provided little history about them. Often explanations were along the lines of, "My husband hasn't touched the instrument in years," "We bought it when our daughter showed a lot of interest but ..." Then they mentioned the considerable amount of money they paid and demanded potential buyers pay what they asked because they wanted to get their investment back. As if keeping a magnificent cello in a closet unused meant its value swelled.

Occasionally, ads included an expensive hard case to protect the instrument, which can cost more than a used beginner-level cello. Many sellers declared their instrument had "great tone." I had a hard time believing dirt-cheap, used cellos available online for a few hundred dollars would guarantee symphony hall–quality sound. The more glorious the verbiage and the clearer and better staged the home photography, the warier I became.

Memories of my dad buying me the cheapest trombone and having me play the instrument for years left me with a lingering psychosis I would never outlive. I wanted to find an instrument that would enhance my ability to play the cello, while remaining within a realistic budget. But where to find it?

At my next lesson, I brought all this up with Mary Ann.

"Oh, yes, there are a lot of cellos out there," Mary Ann said, a little world-weary, as if professional string players were often tossed about on a turbulent sea of cast-off cellos, violins, violas, and basses. Mary Ann went on to advise me that I needed to learn more about cellos before investing in one. My first instinct was to stop paying for the rental, as I couldn't envisage buying a cello at Lake Music simply because they specialize in training students. Higher-end instruments weren't their niche.

"You're going to want to establish a relationship with a specialty store that can help you with repairs, a place with a long history of specializing in strings. They can rehair your bow, make repairs and adjustments, plus they stock different brands of rosin, strings, and whatever else you need. They will even upgrade your instrument as needed," Mary Ann explained.

"Upgrade?" I asked.

"The better stores will let you trade in the cello they sold you for what you paid so you can buy an upgrade."

"What's a decent cello going to cost?" I asked timidly, wondering what I was getting myself into. "I see cellos listed for six hundred dollars online. Used. The people listing them say they're swell." I loved the term "swell" as it reminded me of a bygone age of malt shops and slicked-back hair.

Mary Ann took a deep breath. "Of course they do. You need to play a lot of cellos to compare. You can try out different bows too. Selecting a bow is as important as picking out a cello."

I imagined how all that would work. How could I try out cellos when I could barely play a scale?

"There're places to do this in Portland?" I asked. As I mentioned, Portland has inferiority issues with Seattle, which is located a three-hour drive north, nearly to Canada. For something important, especially a big purchase like this, Portland can have a provincial air that makes me hanker for a bigger, grittier metropolis. For all the rat-a-tat-tat about Portland's screwy boho atmosphere and designer restaurant scene, it's no Paris or Copenhagen. Those of us who've traveled and lived in larger cities get snooty knowing there's a bigger world out there. The feeling was hard to overcome.

"What shall I do?" I asked.

"I think you might start with David Kerr Violin Shop. I've known David for years. More than twenty years—longer than that." Mary Ann pulled out her phone. "I can check their hours."

She called the store. Of course, Mary Ann knew the woman who answered by name.

"I have an adult cello student who'd like to spend some time in the cello room. Try out a lot of different instruments. Doesn't want to buy right now," she added hastily. "Just wants to learn about them."

We were still adjusting to the Covid pandemic petering out, so an online reservation was necessary to visit and spend time in the cello room. This thinned the number of people in the shop at any one time. A mask was still required during a visit as stores slowly relaxed health requirements.

A few days later, Mary Ann met Susan and me at the David Kerr Violin Shop. I thought bringing Susan along was essential so she could experience and better comprehend my burst of interest in the cello, not to mention what she might think about me investing a chunk of change in this endeavor. She'd quickly become accustomed to the cello noises in our house, and this would show her the bigger world of cello music. Also, we both needed to agree to the investment if I was going to buy a cello.

The fabled David Kerr Violin Shop is situated at the corner of a sedate one-way residential street and a neighborhood thoroughfare. The building is unassuming with little to tip it off as the heart of a stringed instrument command center. It has gray wood siding with an awkward parking lot in front and around the back. There isn't a giant violin painted on the front with musical notes. Just a sign with its name.

Reed College is a few blocks down the street. On this campus, a young Steve Jobs famously audited classes for a year or so before heading back to Cupertino to reshape civilization. The neighborhood streets are dotted with restaurants, a classic car emporium, trees, a modest nature preserve, and student apartments.

Mary Ann arrived as we entered through the cello shop's glass front doors. The place was a beehive of instruments. Crammed. Full to the gunwales. Packed like sardines. Cello cases stood upright, crowded together like kids waiting for a bus, filling the entryway with blue, yellow, red, and plenty of black models.

The David Kerr Violin Shop building was originally a bank. All these cases occupied what was once the bank lobby. A long counter ran across the space. To my left was the cello room. I could see through its wall of windows a congregation of cellos lining all four walls. A second cello room for the most expensive instruments was tucked around back—out of reach. The vault with its massive stain-less-steel door slung open, remained from the building's banking days, was full of more string instruments, violins in their cases mostly, lined up like so many library books on shelves. A few elite cellos and larger instruments occupied the vault floor. To protect these from fire or thieves, they simply swing the vault door shut and spin the locking wheel.

The other side of the building's ground floor was divided into sep-arate rooms devoted to violins and violas. The business area stretched into the rear. Behind the counter and up a short staircase sat the busy repair department. From the lobby we caught glimpses of luthiers—

the correct cognomen for instrument builders and technicians—bent over workbenches fixing problems.

Mary Ann and David Kerr were old friends after all their years in music circles around town. Thin and earnest, Kerr had a sense of well-being about him. When he greeted us, I asked how he got into this business. He explained that his mother played cello, so he chose violin to be different. He'd lived in several Oregon towns—started life in Madras, out toward the high desert—but his family moved around.

Kerr learned violin repair in different places to improve his skills. Eventually, he landed at an Ann Arbor, Michigan, violin shop. He was subsequently offered jobs in New York City and Virginia but returned to Portland because he wanted to work for himself. His grandfather owned a lumber business in New Jersey, so he'd always wanted to try running something. Two symphony musicians helped him get started here.

On display were photos from August 1976, when the shop opened. Kerr looked like a college kid with long hair and a beard back then, as did most everybody at that time. A modest counter sat at the entrance to his shop with seemingly little else in his small operation.

"I struggled for the first twenty years. You need lots of gray hair to succeed in this business," he said. "It takes that long to get enough experience to work on these instruments. You have to gain knowledge from all the old antique instruments as they come in. I worked on them for a long time to develop skills. Who wants to bring their two-hundred-year-old cello in, only to discover the luthier doing the repairs has never seen one before? You're not going to feel safe doing that."

Today, Kerr is soft-spoken with a conspicuous calm. He is fluent in cello, violin, and viola, which clearly comes from a deep love of these instruments. Mary Ann, Susan, and I followed him into the cello room, where we listened to Kerr pick out different cellos, telling a little bit about them. He talked about some hidden qualities: mentioning something about the tone of each, where the cello was made, the maker's name, whether the instrument came from a German factory decades ago or more recently from an individual local luthier.

Inside the room, each of the four walls was lined with cellos, standing upright and sideways to us, as if cued up to get into a movie theater. Specially made wooden boxes held them upright, ready for inspection. Some instruments were new. Most were not. I couldn't tell which was which, since new instruments are usually reproductions of the greatest instruments, making them similar to one another. Many, if not most of the cellos, were modeled after Stradivarius designs, as you'd expect, this being the predominate name for quality design. Antonio Stradivari standardized the size of the cello with his Forma B design. Strad violins, and cellos, and other instruments have all been measured, X-rayed, and analyzed for shape, density of the wood, and hidden secrets, including the suspicion that special chemicals were used to treat the wood. Contemporary luthiers try and try again to duplicate his results, even in their cheapest models.

Original Stradivarius violins and cellos and other instruments from hundreds of years ago are indescribably expensive. Some of these premier instruments are loaned to professional musicians. Famously, Yo-Yo Ma has a prized cello of this caliber, which he absent-mindedly left in the trunk of a taxi on his way to a concert in New York. The instrument rode around in the taxi's trunk for hours, unbeknownst to the driver, before being tracked down and returned just in time for Ma to perform.

Musical historians calculate that Stradivari made more than 1,100 instruments, 960 of these being violins, plus harps, violas, and even guitars. He made 80 cellos, of which 63 survive today. Pretty much all these elite instruments are locked safely away in museums or owned by collectors, including corporations that invest in them. Stradivari was born in 1644 and, in time, established a luthier shop in Cremona, Italy. Because his work is widely copied, a label noting an instrument is a Stradivarius or another famous luthier from that era, or having the Cremona name tagged to it, means the instrument is of that style rather than the real McCoy.

Determining the luthier and other information about a cello is often a best guess. To identify the instrument, cellos are supposed to have a paper label glued inside, viewable through the F-hole. The information these gum wrapper–sized pieces of paper provide is painfully brief, usually no more than the luthier's name, where they were located, and the year. When pointing out the labels inside an instrument, Kerr noted that those imported from overseas have had to carry the country of origin since 1891.

He left us alone in the cello room to play a few of these—a daunting task, there were so many. I sat in a chair in the middle with Susan nearby to observe. But where to start? Naturally, Mary Ann had a plan for how to compare one cello to another.

"Let's start along this wall," she said.

Mary Ann went to the west wall and carried over the first cello from the end of the line of reddish-brown rounded shapes.

She hefted each instrument, one at a time, over to me and guided me through the process of giving each one a brief audition. Just to look at any of these cellos all lined up like brown dominos, it was impossible for me to tell much about any of them.

The assessment process began. Mary Ann walked over the first cello and sat in the chair across from me.

"We'll use the same bow on every cello you try to give each one the same opportunity," she explained.

I took the cello handed to me, pulled out the endpin, adjusting the height. This first one didn't feel altogether different from the beat-up student cello I'd been renting. It looked a little less blemished without the general appearance of being ravaged by a noisome and mongrel crew of beginners.

All but one in this room was 4/4, a full-size cello. I suppose I expected all of them to be full size but hadn't given it any thought.

Situating myself with each instrument took a minute, as I still struggled with finding a comfortable way to hold a cello with ease. This was only the second cello I'd ever tried to play. Still, Mary Ann reiterated how she worked to get a good tone from students from the start.

"Speed and pressure. Give it a try," she said.

I pulled the bow across the C string, the bottom note on a cello. This produced an immense, colossal, volcanically large, booming vibration that throbbed the wooden body from its center outward in an explosion of sound. Not a thin note, like my rented student cello made, but rather, layer upon layer of resonance that vibrated my skeleton. How could I have not known my rental cello sounded so weak? My first impression of it seemed so robust.

I lifted the bow smoothly from the string, and the cello continued to ring. Never did I imagine I could coerce so much sound from an instrument with so little effort.

"Are they all like this?" I was impressed by the thick, layered sound a single swipe of the bow made.

"Well, no." Mary Ann smiled as if she'd been waiting to deliver this surprise. "They're all a little different. What we're going to do is try a lot of them so you can make comparisons."

She never said anything negative about the rental I'd been playing. Not directly. But its shortcomings were obvious with what even this first instrument had to offer. How many more could I try out without losing track of which sounded better than the next?

Mary Ann took the first cello, returned it to its base, and asked, "Would you like to consider this one? How did it sound? What do you think?"

"The first is the hardest. I need to make some comparisons," I said.

We quickly developed a system for evaluating each cello, and I started picking them apart. Mary Ann produced a pack of yellow Post-it notes. "We can put one of these on it. Go around the room, sticking one on each cello you think has some potential. Then go back through to refine the search."

"I'll handle the notes." Susan took charge of them, applying one to the base holding the cello I tried first.

There were more than sixty cellos lining the walls all the way around the room. I felt like they were all waiting for their moment, trying to come across just right, the way dancers try out for Broadway shows, hoping they look good. Some seemed smug as they waited their turn. Others had a take-it-or-leave-it attitude. For some reason I sensed a number of them coming across shy and unsure of themselves. One seemed to flirt, seeming to drop a shoulder and wink.

What was going on in my head with this? Next I'd be anthropomorphizing cats, and I'm allergic to cats and stay clear of them.

"Give this a try." Mary Ann brought over the next cello. I tried a scale, using the full length of the bow to make a long pull across each string.

"Try it with more pressure and speed. See what you get," Mary Ann said.

This cello exploded in sound, much like the first. I said, "It's brighter. Sharper and narrower."

Mary Ann nodded. "You're developing a vocabulary. Helpful when comparing qualities, isn't it? How does this compare to the first?"

While all the full-size cellos were essentially the same size, ignoring for the moment my screwy visualizations of them, each had its own distinguishing features. A lighter or darker color, scratches here and there, no evidence of wear, or all beat up. Each felt just different enough when I picked it up. One exploded in richness while another offered something thinner, more tentative. Their personalities emerged in ways I did not expect.

Susan placed yellow notes on the next two cellos. Then I started to get picky. I didn't want to go through all of them again. First impressions made a difference, became much more important in winnowing out instruments as we worked along the wall. My approach evolved as I grew less impressed with the first feeling of depth from a note. I went looking for faults, shortcomings, whether the cello played as well soft as loud. Did I need to coax a richer tone from the particular cello, or did it appear all on its own? All that. Everything I could think of. Every quality Mary Ann mentioned I should look for.

Susan stayed pretty quiet during this process without any particular opinion on the tone on any of them, though she did mention the finish on one. "The wood is wavy on the back," she said.

Good point. Different woods can be used to make a cello. Each type will respond in ways that give a cello its own character. Even slight variations in the grain or quality of the wood can steer the sound around one way or another. Make the sound high or sweet. Round out the tone at the bottom. Variations in the way these cellos played seemed endless as I moved from one to the next.

Because the instruments made by the masters have hundreds of years on them, they are dinged and spotted. Varnish can yellow, darken, crack. Spots appear. Cellos fall over, are dropped, cracked. Some are taken apart, have parts replaced, are reassembled and improved. Or sadly, disastrously rebuilt, deadening the sound.

Contemporary cello luthiers too often distress the outside to give an antique look. Just the way Disneyland stipples paint on the Adventureland buildings to falsely age them or adds creaky boards to the Indiana Jones ride to help you imagine you're making a journey to a faraway land.

When a cello looks weathered, as though it's been a remarkable audience-pleaser for a long time, some people see this as an essential quality that enhances performance. Not all cellos are finished so they appear antique from the start. Some new instruments are left to age naturally over time. I prefer these, finding new cellos with artificial aging a little screwy. Instruments ought to accumulate scratches and dings as most things do, by being accidently banged into something or dropped, along with whatever other day-to-day catastrophes they encounter.

Or there's a more direct musical comparison of how musicians and their instruments look. In an interview with Peter Noone, who fronted Herman's Hermits, a British Invasion band, talked about getting interested in rock and roll when he was just a kid. He saved up and made his mum take him to the shoe store.

"I want a pair of boots with Spanish heels," he insisted. These are thick-heeled boots flamenco dancers wear, the same boot style the Beatles wore at the time.

"Why on earth would you want to wear those?" Noone's mum asked, studying a pair in the store.

He tried them on while dressed in his school uniform—short pants, a jacket, and cap. His mum took a look at him. Block-heel black boots with the shorts and uniform looked out of whack.

"Are you daft?" she said. "You can't go out in public looking like that!"

"I need them to perform with my band," the future Hermit's singer insisted. "Spanish heels make you a better guitar player."

It was all a matter of look for this musician.

Many brand-new cellos come antiqued to suggest they have a heritage. Others simply appear new because they are. A new or newer instrument would show its age as it actually aged, I thought.

"Look inside." Mary Ann had been doing this, though I hadn't caught on. "On the label inside is the luthier's name. Usually the date and model."

I laid the next cello on my lap, and peered through one of the F-holes for the label. There was the rectangular piece of paper glued flat. This label was parchment with mouse type. A magnifying glass is worthless in this situation. If I'd brought my bird-watching binoculars, I'd have given those a try to read what was there.

Even when I could make out most of what the inscription said, some interpretation was required. Many indicated the cellos were "Stradivarius," usually meaning based on a Strad model Forma B. Others said "Cremona," the name of the town where many famous luthiers' workshops were located, suggesting dynastic origins. A handful were made in the United States. A few came from individual luthiers whose cello output would always remain small. Their shops, which were often out of their homes, might have produced three or four instruments a year.

Sometimes they make violins and an occasional viola. Basses are a different animal and treated in an entirely separate category from violins, violas, and cellos. There were no upright string basses in this shop.

We worked our way around the room using Mary Ann's system. Eventually, she started skipping one or two along the way. There were just too many to try. If I tested out too many all at once, the whole experience would devolve into a blur, leaving me unable to tell one candidate from another.

Susan tagged the instruments that stood out for one reason or another, but even then, there were more than I thought I could manage. Perhaps twenty cellos gained yellow Post-it notes by the time we got around the cello room. I was exhausted.

We asked David Kerr back into the room, reintroducing his calming presence. Kerr had been around stringed instruments so long they were old friends to him. Each had a different personality and heritage. He knew each one, or at least had some background on most of them—the luthier, origin, or how his shop came to have it. He could readily compare instruments with this knowledge.

"All the yellow stickers mark instruments to try again. Compare and contrast." Mary Ann pointed around to them.

Kerr nodded in his Yoda-like presence.

"What do these cost?" I asked, broaching the most obvious constraint when purchasing anything. None of the prices were marked.

"An expensive cello doesn't necessarily sound better than a less expensive model," he said.

Kerr went to the wall behind Mary Ann where we had begun and pointed down the row. "These start at $2,500 and go up to $5,000." Going clockwise around the room, Kerr swept his hand along the next wall, the one behind me. "These are $5,000 to $10,000. In that range."

He pulled out one of the two German cellos resting next to one another in that lineup. "These are good. German factory instruments helped a lot of students start out. For the last twenty years though, Chinese instruments have shown so much improvement, they're setting a new standard for quality, playability, tone. They're affordable."

"Chinese cellos?" I asked. "What changed?"

Mary Ann leaned into the explanation. "Early Chinese violins were shoeboxes. Cardboard. Unplayable. The edges weren't finished. They were just terrible excuses for violins, cellos, violas, whatever they were shipping over here."

"I'd always assumed that quality string instruments were European because that's where the cello and violin originated," I offered.

"Traditionally, that's been the case, but the Chinese product has improved greatly," Kerr said. He picked out a few more cellos, after that. gave a story for each, and talked about the maker, the origin country, and usually the price. Though he had to look up a couple prices to be sure.

A couple instruments were made in the United States. Two in particular came from the shops of Oregon luthiers. One shop seemed to have closed down. The other, Kerr described as having the best tone in the cello room.

"This is from a luthier in McMinnville, Kile Hill. He's a newcomer, a rising star, and once word gets around about him, he's going to get very busy." Kerr had a sense of awe saying this. Proud a local cello studio made quality instruments.

McMinnville, Oregon, is forty-five minutes west of Portland, surrounded by rolling hills dotted with wineries. McMinnville is also home to Howard Hughes's Spruce Goose, which is displayed in an air museum with an indoor waterpark. It is also where cellos are made by experienced luthiers with a great deal of training, apprenticeship, time, and patience, as well as quality wood and tools. They were not cheap. I liked the idea that these were being made nearby.

We were into our second hour working through the cello room. Kerr finished explaining that the third and fourth walls in the room had cellos in the higher price range, up to around $40,000. I didn't need such an expensive instrument at this point in my cello playing. Obviously, we would limit our focus going forward to the least expensive wall. Mary Ann led me through an elimination process, of these cellos and Susan wrangled the yellow notes as we winnowed them out.

"All right. Ready?" Mary Ann went over to the less expensive wall again, brought one back, and played the instrument. "Try it with a lot of pressure, then again softly."

I followed her directions. The more instruments I compared, the quicker I could eliminate any that seemed to fight me when I played them. If the strings were too high off the fingerboard, causing the action to become too cumbersome, I took the sticker off. On one, the varnish appeared to have yellowed and felt rough, so I eliminated that instrument.

"Don't look inside this time so you don't know the maker," Mary Ann said, handing me another cello. "Start closing your eyes when you play so you can listen with more focus."

I did all this. Started comparing one cello to another more critically. Played one. Handed the cello to Mary Ann, who handed me a different cello. Gave that one a try, then returned to the one I'd tried before. A quick camaraderie developed with some of the instruments I tried and less so with others. It reminded me of picking friends, which usually begins by discovering who you get along with easily.

Susan removed the yellow notes when an instrument was eliminated, and soon enough, we were down to three cellos. I tried each of these again, one after the other, eyes closed, eyes open, thoroughly examining how the wood and varnish looked. I held the instrument in playing position, feeling the vibe as I played. But I didn't look inside to find out who made them.

In the end, I picked the cello I felt was superior to all those on the wall of least expensive offerings. On the last one, the tone filled the room and might even be able to fill an auditorium. This cello was the best overall. We asked Kerr to come back in and talk about this instrument.

Naturally, the cello I selected was the most expensive in that first group. I looked inside. The label said: Fiammato—Handmade in China. Level 5. Anno 2022.

The instrument was new, level 5 being top of the line for this manufacturer. Just as both David Kerr and Mary Ann said, Chinese instruments had improved. Having tried so many that morning, it seemed they sure had. *Fiammato* means flamed because the maple used on the sides and back displayed a rippled pattern that looked like flames.

"That's a good instrument for you to begin with. What about a bow?" Kerr asked.

A bow not being included hadn't occurred to me. Didn't that just come along, like grits with your eggs in Nashville? You're saying it's extra? They'd give me an inexpensive bow to get started, but it wasn't one they'd recommend.

Mary Ann could see I was not ready to evaluate something else. I wouldn't be checking out bows, at least not right now. I looked exhausted, felt spent, and could not start evaluating the virtues of different bows today.

"We can look at bows down the road," she said.

Susan approved of my selection of cello and encouraged me to go ahead with it. While I hadn't come to buy, only to look and familiarize myself, I took the instrument home to try free for a week. After playing it every day until feeling comfortable with the selection, I arranged to buy my first cello on a three-month payment plan.

Chapter 12
Here Comes the Sun

On my fifth lesson, I walked my old, tired rental cello through the front door of Lake Music and handed it in. Then I returned to my car to retrieve my new instrument and carried it in with a strut in my step. As my new cello and I strolled by my former cello sitting on the floor, it looked forlorn, sadly abandoned once more by another student who'd quickly outgrown it. How many times had it been dumped like this before?

Mary Ann arrived for our lesson as I lifted my new cello from its case. It felt weightless, though its tonnage was probably within an ounce of the student model I'd been using. Once I got into the teeny tiny lesson studio with Mary Ann, I set up the cello, took my bow, then did a grip-and-rip, using speed and pressure on the bow across the string. The bellowing C note vibrated my knees, thighs, legs, ribcage, skull, arms, entire skeleton. It rattled the windows and knocked the peeling paint from the showroom wall and probably shingles off the leaky roof.

I'd seen a documentary that followed Paul McCartney when he visited the flat his family rented where he grew up. He showed the audience the family's bathroom where he went to play. He sat on the toilet, lid down of course, to show how the little washroom gave his guitar playing an energizing, bright sound. He'd practiced there.

Same thing happened in Mary Ann's little studio.

"Grip it and rip it," she reiterated.

The cello's robust sound bounced off the little room's walls. Working up the strings, C, G, D, A, this cello gave me what I missed—a fulfilling sense of a beautiful, rich, deep pool at the bottom of a waterfall. This was the sound that had compelled me to play by providing the rich feeling of being alive. Wasn't this what I'd responded to when I heard the lecturer play in Spain?

I talked with Mary Ann about my desire to play my favorite song on the cello. Cello music for "Here Comes the Sun" was easy to find on the web, and I downloaded a copy for a couple bucks. We took a look at the sheet music, and she had me sight-read the first page, which I was able to work my way through ever so slowly. Having gone through the process of buying my own cello, I wanted to learn more about how the instrument was made and why the best cellos got that reputation.

"Maybe I could make playing this song on a really good cello a goal?" I said.

"Sure, there are plenty of good cellos around," Mary Ann said.

"Where can I find a Stradivarius?"

"In a museum. He didn't make that many of them."

"Have you played one, I mean, ever played a Stradivarius violin?" I asked.

"Yes, several," she said casually, as if it were no big deal. "At a professional level, you might attend workshops or conferences where they have those to play. You have to have some credentials to get your hands on a Strad, but it's not impossible."

"Where would I go looking?" I asked.

"The Smithsonian for one. I attended a workshop there and played a Strad violin for half an hour."

"But you need to be approved, probably?" I asked.

"I would think so," Mary Ann answered. "Something important to remember: Instruments are meant to be played. It's a tragedy to have great and important instruments in a collection and never hear them played."

There it was. Another goal. Stradivarius has the reputation for creating the best string instruments of all time, and I wanted to play a particular song on one. A Stradivarius cello just to see if magic would happen the way it did listening to the master cellist in Spain that amazing evening. Were Strads as supernatural and charmed as their reputation suggests?

I decided to find out.

Search for a Strad

Most mornings I'm up at six. My iPhone plays a subdued wake-up tune. I sit up in bed, while drinking a cup of something Susan makes using our electric kettle. This kettle is a fast and sophisticated addition to our kitchen. There are settings to use, so the kettle heats water to the perfect temperature for black, green, or other teas, all very fast—much faster than a whistling pot on a stove.

These morning rituals are important. I gave up on coffee after drinking hundreds of thousands of gallons over the years. I tried tea for a while before shifting to Droste, an unsweetened cacao powder, famous for the picture of an infinitely repeating image of a Dutch nurse on the box. It's made in the Netherlands. There's no sugar or caffeine in Droste.

Sipping a cup while sitting in bed, I check the bank balances, pay bills on my laptop, and write a list of what I intend to accomplish that day, including what I forgot about and now remember from the lists of days ago. This usually includes a note to practice the cello and exercise one way or another too, which translates to walking five miles a day if I can talk myself into it, along with whatever I'm writing or researching. Sometimes I number the list to create a momentary sense of urgency.

That morning, I hoped to set up meetings with some new experts for my cello research. I hadn't heard back from the Smithsonian about their instrument collection after several attempts to contact them. Weeks had gone by while I sent emails to the Smithsonian and left a couple of phone messages. Since Mary Ann had mentioned the Smithsonian string collection in glowing terms, I thought I'd give them a try.

"It's a classy operation. Really first rate," Mary Ann had said.

However, they'd skunked me so far. Perhaps access to the curators was restricted to professional musicians or notable scholars. To them, I assumed, I was just some old, gnarly dude in Oregon with a cello obsession. Still, if I could connect with the right Smithsonian expert, I could have a conversation to find out more about cello history, which would lead to what else I needed to learn. There was my determination to play "Here Comes the Sun," my favorite song from my days of installing the new cassette deck, on a Strad, but it was looking like Washington, D.C., wouldn't be the place I could do it. Wasn't that where the Strads were?

The Smithsonian websites contain libraries of knowledge. They operate twenty museums, plus additional collections, traveling shows, and the National Zoo. Some of the online information goes into excruciating detail, while other parts are full of gee-whiz facts for kids and easily digestible presentations for exploration by adults. Like all expansive websites, there are plenty of dead ends, out-of-date info, and duplicate pages.

Over the last couple months, I scoured the web for contact information related to instruments in different museums. Most of the time, when I requested to be put in touch with the best person to talk to about cellos, I received an automated response apologizing for being overwhelmed by inquiries and informing me I might not get a response. When an unsigned response from the Smithsonian did arrive after a long wait, it said they "didn't think [they] could help me with my request for information on the subject I inquired about."

Still, I figured the reason I failed to connect with the right people must be that I hadn't put enough energy into the search. It wasn't focused enough.

That morning, as I sipped Droste, sitting in bed with my laptop searching "Smithsonian cello" and related terms on DuckDuckGo, I came across the Smithsonian Chamber Music Society. The name was a little different from the other Smithsonian Museum pages I'd found.

The society's homepage showcased classical musicians dressed in sober-looking suits, earnestly playing string instruments—violins, violas, and cellos. It appeared at first glance that their concerts were in only Washington, D.C. I had not uncovered this organization before.

I searched and searched, finally locating a contact form, then dashed off a brief email asking, "Who's the best person to talk to about cellos?" When I sent the email, I figured it would bounce around the internet for a while before disappearing like my other requests.

I took another sip of my new Dutch beverage and moved on to the next bright, shiny thing on the internet. Two minutes and thirty-three seconds later, at 7:21 a.m. Pacific time, my phone rang. The caller ID said Smithsonian. I fumbled the phone.

"Hello?" I gasped.

"Hello, George, this is (some name that went by too fast to catch) from the Smithsonian." The man's chipper voice sounded energized and positive and interested. "How can I help you with the book you're writing?"

Bedazzled, I replied, "That was fast."

He laughed. "Right. I see you get up early, so I just called."

I rushed to organize my thoughts. It was midmorning back East and brave of him to pick up the phone just like that. "Who is the best person to talk with at the Smithsonian about the cello?"

"That would be me," the man said. How disarming to hear this refreshing tone of confidence and interest. But with whom was I talking?

"Do you play the cello?" I asked.

"Since I was four years old," he said.

From there, we covered hundreds of years of cello history, an overview of the Smithsonian collection, the joy of feeling the vibration of the instrument when you play, and how natural and ergonomic playing the cello is compared to the violin. This is because the violin requires holding your left hand and arm in such an unnatural position.

"Did you know," he said, "it's reported that if a violinist doesn't start playing by age seven, they probably will never reach a high level of excellence because they need flexibility that's developed from their youth?"

All this amazing information came so fast I couldn't absorb everything. I asked if we could talk the next day so I could properly prepare.

"Sure," he said. I had him spell his name, and we agreed to speak again early the following morning.

By the time I got to my 1:30 cello lesson with Mary Ann, I'd looked into whom I had talked with. I shared his name with my teacher.

"Kenneth Slowik called me this morning," I mentioned in passing. "He's the artistic director of the Smithsonian Chamber Music Society."

I managed to mispronounce his name. After Mary Ann's eyes popped open, she steadied herself in the lesson room chair and correctly annunciated his name, adding some information.

"Kenneth Slowik is one of the premier cello players in the world—a legend."

"When he called me this morning, I asked him if he played the cello," I said. "He said he'd been playing for something like one hundred years."

"He's a magnificent cellist, pianist, musician, historian—many recordings. You spoke with a class act." Mary Ann opened her hands to the tiny teaching space. "My humble room is not able to bear it."

Early the next morning, I spoke with Kenneth Slowik again, this time prepared for the conversation. First thing, I made it clear I knew his accomplishments, explained my surprise at getting his call, all with my total appreciation for him taking the time to talk. I was, after all, simply a senior adult beginner writing about the experience.

"A big part of our job here at the Smithsonian is serving the public," he said with vim.

"Why am I so interested in playing the cello all of a sudden, at seventy-one?" I asked. Why not start out with that unexpected question I love asking, since I haven't been able to fully understand it myself?

"You have an affinity for the sound of it. It has the range and timbre of the human voice. The cello is more ergonomic than many instruments. The flute has a funny embouchure. Oboe, the same. The violin, I mentioned yesterday, you raise up at your side, arms in the air, with an awkward elbow. Holding the cello, you become one with it," Slowik said.

This was what I'd observed on the Camino from the Spanish professor when I watched him play. How he merged with the instrument.

I answered, "I'm just getting past figuring out what angle to hold the cello, how to get my knees on the sides. I watch videos of players to study them, but there's no one way they do it."

"Everybody is differently proportioned—length of legs, longer or shorter arms—it's like a well-trodden path across a field when you become comfortable with how to hold a cello. Isn't that great?" Slowik said encouragingly. "Each player figures it out for their self. After about ten thousand hours, it gets easier. The more you play, the greater the rewards."

Slowik explained he began playing instruments at four years old, starting with the piano, before moving to cello lessons with a locally known violin player in his hometown, Chicago. He took to the cello and improved to the point where his teacher said she'd taken him as far as she could, recommending he audition for a cello teacher to see if she'd accept him as a student.

The young cellist played a Bach suite. The whole time the instructor watched him play with unusual intensity. Turned out he'd played the piece using violin technique. Slowik had to relearn what he'd been taught to accommodate the cello. Violins are different. A violin is smaller, and the way they're tuned is different. The violin uses diatonic fingering while the cello is chromatic.

The cello evolved from larger instruments than the violin. Violoncello is the official full name, though everyone calls it the cello. Likewise, the piano's full name is pianoforte, but who calls it that? For a long time, the cello had no endpin. You had to clamp it in a death grip between your calves. The Smithsonian collection includes some of these historic instruments. The Smithsonian Chamber Music Society even gives performances using them.

Slowik encouraged me to look at seventeenth-century Dutch paintings with cellos in them. The instruments were bigger then. Sometimes you see the cello sitting on stacks of pillows or on a stool while played because of the lack of an endpin to raise them. The 1676 Thomas Mace book, *Musik's Monument*, describes this as a practice technique, he explained.

After becoming proficient, players would hold their instrument between their knees at the time. Gladly, the endpin became popular by the twentieth century. Even so, some cellists played without this spike holding up the bottom of the cello into the early 1900s.

Slowik explained how instruments evolved. The viola da spalla is a small cello or large viola hung by a strap over the player's neck, played with a bow so big it looks like Robin Hood could use it to shoot arrows at the Sheriff of Nottingham. There's also the viola da gamba—called the gamba most of the time. This is the predecessor of today's cello. There's been an evolution in string instruments since the dawn of time.

There is no way I could absorb all the nuances of the stringed instruments, shape changes, sizes ballooning larger and shrinking over the centuries. Certainly not during one mesmerizing phone call. Basically, today's cello developed during the first half of the sixteenth century as violin luthiers began a reinvention of that instrument when it became wildly popular. He reminded me that cello design stabilized with Stradivari landing on the Forma B design. This is the cello design against which all cellos are compared.

Like so many of us, I learn by seeing and doing, instead of listening to lectures or reading about things. Much to Slowik's credit, I followed along with his narrative, as the way he described things made them easy to understand. I still looked forward to at least seeing the Smithsonian's cellos—and hearing them, if possible—to understand what the musicians who first played them and the luthiers tweaking the designs were working toward.

"What guidance can you give me starting out? I have a new cello, and I'm getting into a practice routine," I said.

"Think about breaking in your cello," he said. He explained that the cello needs to vibrate. A cello has a fantastic sound, and you can warm up by playing your cello loud and out of tune.

"Play it out of tune on purpose, not by accident the way I do now," I said.

"Play your open G string, then play a G on the C string. Place your fourth finger on the fourth position, which is another G, right?"

"Right," I agreed.

"Then move your finger up or down the fingerboard so you hear a harmonic wave. *Wa-ah-wa-ah-wa-ah*," Slowik said. "Understand?"

"I'll try it."

"It'll tell you a lot about your instrument. It's a good warm-up," he explained.

People have five fingers on each hand, until they start playing cello. Then their left hand becomes four fingers and a thumb. The index finger is one, middle finger two, ring finger three, with the pinkie number four. When told to place my fourth finger in the fourth position to play a G note on the C string, it was pretty straightforward, even for me.

Trying this, I played a G on both strings at the same time, and by moving my pinkie just a little out of position, I bowed the strings, and the cello responded with a robust *wa-ah-wa-ah-wa-ah* that seemed it could shake the instrument apart.

Finally, I asked how to produce the best tone from a cello. "My teacher says it's speed and pressure of the bow," I explained.

Slowik said there was one more part to this. "Contact point. This is the position where the bow intersects the strings. The closer to the bridge you play, the greater the chance of a whistling sound. Find the spot on your cello that gives you the best sound; that's the contact point."

Mary Ann had said the same thing with just a little different emphasis.

In thanking Kenneth Slowik for taking time to go over all this with an old beginner, I asked if I could follow up and come out to see the Smithsonian historic instrument collection in the summer.

"Of course, glad to answer any questions. It's too far out to make an appointment for July. Just contact me close to the date," Slowik exclaimed. "Keep practicing! Goodbye!"

This was an astonishing phone call.

The Smithsonian has two Stradivarius cellos in their collection—the Marylebon and the Servais. The Marylebon cello is part of the Axelrod quartet of Stradivarius instruments. These were collected by Herbert R. Axelrod and generously donated to the museum to preserve and play.

The quartet is made up of the Greffuhle violin, Axelrod viola, Ole Bull violin, and Marylebon cello. Ole Bull was a legendary Norwegian violin virtuoso and composer.

The list of the cellos made by Antonio Stradivari that still exist somewhere in the world shows they are in museums or private hands, with some of these elegant instruments on loan to professional musicians.

There are interesting stories about some of the Stradivarius cellos on the list. The Mara Stradivarius cello went down with a Montevideo-to-Buenos Aires ferry after the ferry caught fire and sank. The instrument was eventually recovered from the depths and rebuilt. The Amaryllis Fleming cello had been owned by the half-sister of James Bond creator Ian Fleming before being auctioned off. She was a celebrated cellist, and the concert hall at the Royal College of Music was named in her honor.

The Smithsonian's Marylebon was made by Antonio Stradivari in 1688, in Cremona, Italy. It was named for a neighborhood in London but spelled without an E at the end used in Great Britain. Interestingly, it was reduced in size, and in the nineteenth century, further decorated to imitate what was thought to be Stradivari's ornamentation.

The Servais cello was built in 1701. This cello is named for François Servais, who owned it from about 1840. It is considered the best, most beautiful-sounding cello in the world. The instrument is large. In the years after its creation, Stradivarius made slightly smaller cellos or cut down the instruments he had on hand, as is the case with the Marylebon. But the Servais was saved from this alteration and remains its original larger size.

Chapter 13
Exploring the Wilderness

Once I bought my own cello, my lessons became more focused, as if having made this purchase made me all the more serious, with the new cello there to prove it. I'd head over to Lake Music and get set up in the studio for a lesson. Mary Ann would say, "Here's what I have planned for this lesson." Then she'd observe something about my playing, and we'd go from there.

"You're bobbing back and forth. You don't need to do that. Don't tap your feet. Your expression says you're racked with torment," she said, referring to the way I looked during sections where I'd get lost or screw up the fingering. "But that will go away. Just be aware you're doing it." I took these nudges as small course corrections.

On other occasions, I'd wouldn't feel comfortable in the chair and take on ungainly postures.

"Relax your shoulders, they're too tense. Adjust the endpin, and lower your shoulders."

I shortened the endpin, lowering the cello.

"Good, that brought them down. Now check the angle of the cello. Is it too upright or angled down too much? Consider what's most comfortable for you."

During another lesson, Mary Ann might say the opposite. "You're bent over too much. Let out the endpin all the way so you'll sit up." There was more of a physical workout than I'd imagined.

Mary Ann's corrections speak to my posture, how I am sitting in relation to the instrument. In some pictures of me playing, I look bent over the thing. Others have me leaned back. The position of the tuning pegs is by my ear in some photos, while in others behind my head. This leads to the discussion about what sort of seat you're on.

On a stool, you have to sit up straight with no spine support. You have to have good posture—a struggle for me. I prefer a chair I can lean back on. Though some will say you don't need to lean back, and a cellist ought to be seated forward on a chair while sitting upright. I sought out a couple professional cellists I sought out a couple professional cellists to learn how they came to play professionally and to talk about chairs. None of them had a solid answer to this—it was to each their own. Do whatever's comfortable for you, they all told me.

When I practiced, I pulled over a dining table chair. The wooden seats were as hard as granite, so I'd borrow a couch pillow to sit on. This felt more comfortable while raising me higher in relation to the cello. This started a search for the right chair. Did professional cellists have a preferred chair to sit on when they played? A perfect seat or stool? I watched videos of Yo-Yo Ma (as you'd suspect) and other cello greats performing, hoping to learn what chair they sit on while they play. There is a cavalcade of videos from amateurs and pros about all things cello, but I could find nothing specifically about a cello chair.

I tried to figure out the way pros handled seating by studying how high they were sitting in relation to the cello, the cello angle, how far back the tuning pegs were behind their ear. I watched dozens of videos of performances, lessons, and workshops, and some dealing with individual compositions, especially the "Prelude" for *Suite 1* from Bach's *Six Suites for the Cello*.

It seemed I should sit higher, as I'm six feet, one inch tall—or was before starting to shrink—and have seen some cellists appear to sit higher than a regular chair would offer. Some were on stools. Whether or not they were special cello stools became a mystery I wanted solved. These little things bothered me, a beginner, much more than they do someone who's been playing for a long time and gotten past all the distractions.

I mentioned the chair business at a lesson. Soon, Mary Ann located a three-dollar artist stool with a low back at a secondhand store for me to try. The stool had a low back and plenty of height, basically a bar stool you'd use at home. She's a pawn shop–thrift store hound who knows where to find these things. I tried it a few times and ended up cutting an inch or so off the legs, continuing to try it out to adjust the height.

"You're an adult student, so I don't have to tell you to play every day. Play as much as you can get yourself to," Mary Ann had said.

"Keep making adjustments until you find some equilibrium, some comfortable position that makes the cello easier."

As the lessons continued, Mary Ann showed up covered in dog hair. The back of her sweater had so much light-colored fur it glowed. I didn't have to ask why. Her Labrador puppy had been spayed, so Mary Ann spent days afterward on the floor, holding the dog's paw and apologizing for the trouble. I knew this, since she had been relentlessly chronicling the event on social media. Mary Ann took a lot of selfies with the forlorn puppy and posted them.

I did not mention to her directly anything about her being covered with dog hair, as cello players are always polite and supportive of one another.

With a few months of lessons, I got into a routine. I would arrive at Lake Music, and start unpacking my instrument, and warming up in the store. This was an uneven experience as the furnace was out on this end of the building, though the Costa Rican restaurant had a new system recently installed. In winter it would get icy cold. I took a seat from one of the electric pianos on display to run scales and noodle around on my cello. During my lesson, my cello case remained in the store as there was no room in the lesson studio or along the narrow corridor.

When Mary Ann arrived, she'd say, "Let's get this lesson going."

Because of her knee issues, she doddered a little but with a lot of energy over to her lesson studio and unlocked the door if the young guy on duty at the register hadn't already opened it. He provided a list of students for that day. I was usually the first lesson, at one o'clock. Sometimes there was another student, a woman around my age, who took a violin lesson after me. The parade of learners who followed us were school-age students for the most part. Mary Ann typically gave lessons until eight in the evening, managing her way through a long day of teaching, often involving fourteen or so students.

Once Mary Ann situated herself, I would move chairs around and get the backless bench out of the way so I could use a standard wooden chair. Sometimes I remembered to bring a couch pillow from home to use on the hard seat, allowing me to sit a little higher because I'd seen cellists my size seated comfortably at a more elevated position.

Sometimes we faced the grated windows overlooking the parking lot. Other times we oriented ourselves toward the open door. The small, cluttered room offered few options. At one point, a couple months into this, Mary Ann's phone was regularly pinging a message alert. She'd managed to get on multiple lists for relentless political fundraising, seemingly for every party that's ever existed. In addition to breaking news, friends checking in, and weather alerts. I made her turn off all notifications.

For a while, we began lessons with routine warm-up scales while trying to vibrato each note. The results of learning to vibrato notes sounds great when done right, but takes time to master, as the mechanics of wiggling the left hand with one finger on a string to create vibrato involves your entire arm. After a few minutes up and down a C scale, if Mary Ann had a lesson plan, which she sort of did, we would go on with that.

"There are different levels of understanding when it comes to playing the cello," she said. "As you play, ask yourself if the instrument resonates. Does it allow you to play, or does it fight you? This isn't necessarily the cello that's responsible for not giving you what you want, it can be the player. How can you make what you're playing more musical? Make the notes flow from one to the next. There's the flow of the notes as you move effortlessly from one element of playing to another." She spoke with calm and experience, as if nothing about playing music could surprise her.

As the lessons moved into the next months, I became more comfortable handling the instrument, gaining more skill at hitting the correct spot on the fingerboard, while keeping the bow better positioned on the strings. Mary Ann would take me down the fingerboard, into the higher notes I hadn't used, as though on a journey to a foreign land with few landmarks to navigate the way. Most of the fingering for the first months of lessons stayed toward the top of the fingerboard. The more I studied cellists in person and on videos, the more I saw how using more of the fingerboard made sense. It meant the player didn't need to make as many string crossings. You could play higher notes more quickly and with less effort.

I started with the lowest string, the C string, and played down the fingerboard—following the C scale—note after note.

"Move up a note," Mary Ann said as I worked my finger down a string, since that makes the string shorter and the pitch higher. Down is up. "Eventually you will play more of the fingerboard. Slide down a step. Listen to find where your finger goes. When you move down to where the neck joins the body of the cello, place your thumb on the string to help the finger in front hold down the string."

I continued to play down each string like this. The A string, which is the highest pitched, felt at first like I'd been walking a smooth, well-maintained trail. When I moved down the fingerboard on that string, which would take me to the highest notes on the cello, I felt like I was hitting the shrieking stratosphere. The notes sounded more like an unoiled door hinge than a musical scale. While your fingers go down the fingerboard, taking the scale higher and higher, the notes move into the range of the violin. This adventure felt like exploring a wilderness, then reaching a point where you have to backtrack or you'll get hopelessly lost.

The higher you move up in pitch, the distance between notes shrinks, the tone thins out, and your thumb or another finger help out, so two fingers are holding down the string as the note is played. Just to make things complicated, these high notes can sometimes be played by touching the string without pushing it to the fingerboard to achieve a harmonic.

Imagine a piano built so that the higher up the scale you play, the narrower the piano keys become. That's how the cello is set up.

"You're learning the full range available. You'll eventually find these notes a help," Mary Ann said.

"I'm understanding the sharps and flats are hidden in there between the real notes," I said.

"Right. The real notes. You have a good ear. You're adjusting your finger to the correct pitch. You hear this?" she said.

"Yes, it's getting easier. Why don't they put frets on the cello the way they do on guitars?" I asked. "That'd make it easier."

"Obviously, cellos are a smart-person instrument," she said.

"There's no simple way to find the positions for each note?" I looked across the fingerboard, which appears as a mile of empty bad road when searching for the exact spot where an F-sharp eighth-note might pop up in the middle of nowhere.

Mary Ann made a donut with an index finger. "You've got to put your finger right on that dot."

Toward the end of each lesson, I would pull out my music for "Here Comes the Sun," and we'd spend some time on that. The cello version I'd found did not have the intro section, which on the recording is a guitar solo ending with the ebullient slide down the scale to start the song. Recreating that head-under-the-Volvo-dashboard moment demanded that prodigious, downward sliding note. I figured how to do all this so this section of the Harrison tune was recognizable, at least to me.

Chapter 14
The Luthiers

Quality factory-made cellos, like the one I bought, can have good tone, play well, and offer good value. They sell for a relatively modest price. Their look, sound, and feel promise a positive experience. Now that I played what's considered an entry-level instrument, and with the benefit of getting used to my new cello over some weeks, I wondered what goes into making an even better instrument. How is the cello I play truly different from a top-of-the-line cello? How would it stand up to a Strad or, more realistically, even a quality custom instrument made today? It isn't just that the classic instruments are centuries older that make them better, is it?

All this started me thinking about what is it that differentiates what I play from a quality, handmade model with an eye-popping price? I started by searching for the luthiers who make cellos, wondering how many of them lived near me in the Pacific Northwest. Would their instruments compete with any in the world? Sound vibrant and alive? Be a joy to play and able to deliver a great performance?

I'd heard about luthiers near where I live and wondered if I could visit them to learn more about how cellos are made. How would their creations stack up to the cello gods of Cremona: Amanti, Guarneri, Stradivari, and others? Wouldn't this peel back some of the mystery about how a cello can produce such moving music?

Kile Edward Hill—Luthier

First time I heard of luthier Kile Hill was when his name popped up while auditioning cellos at David Kerr's shop. During a pause in trying out one instrument after another, Kerr came into the room with a cello from the premium instrument room.

"Try this one. I think it has the best tone of any cello we have in stock right now."

He handed me the instrument, and even though I was blurry from interacting with a vast assemblage of cellos, I tried this one, giving it a lot of attention.

The cello felt comfortable.

"Good cellos are easy to play," Mary Ann reminded me.

Hill's cello played as if it were cooperating with me. I sensed I didn't have to work so hard at producing a quality, articulate tone—this cello just provided one. A superior instrument, of course, costs more. Leaving with this cello was out of my grasp. Being a beginner, I could set my sights on owning this cello one day. Probably when I became a better player. Still, I was impressed that Mr. Kerr himself would present Hill's cello in this way.

What makes one cello that much better than another? Part of this must be the way an individual player interacts with a particular instrument and how they understand its personality. There aren't that many parts to a cello, are there? Wood is the main component. Maple and spruce are the most frequently used woods. They are carefully selected, then left to dry for a long time. There's glue to hold it all together, some hardware such as tuning pegs, strings, an endpin. Not much more than that. If this is all you need, what happens in a luthier's shop, or cello factory for that matter, where one maker creates a cheap and unresponsive tub of wood, while another creates a miracle of cordiality that is a rabble-rousing joy to play?

"Kile Hill works out of McMinnville, has his shop there. Once he becomes better known, there's going to be strong demand for his instruments," Kerr had said.

Why wouldn't I want to track down a successful cello luthier to find out how a great cello is created? McMinnville is in Oregon's wine country, a forty-five-minute drive west from Portland. The rolling hills and shallow valleys are swathed in grape vines, oaks, and pine trees.

I was able to meet with Hill at Durant Winery, near his home where he operates a cello workshop. He felt it easier to meet at the winery, and I recommended Durant because Susan works there three days a week, so I knew the place. She thought guests would be interested to have a cello mysteriously appear on a busy weekend.

The Durant operation provided plenty of room to talk, but is also distinctive, as it operates the only olive oil mill in the Pacific Northwest. During this rainy spring Sunday, they had a tent set up adjacent to their boutique farm shop with a variety of infused olive oils to taste. At the opposite end of their property, Durant has an indoor space for tasting wine. That building is situated at the crest of a hill, and on a clear day, there are hundred-mile views of snow-covered Mount Hood and Mount Jefferson, and a good stretch of the rippling Cascade Range.

There is also a nursery with olive trees and other plants for sale. Olive trees and Oregon wouldn't seem to go together weather-wise. However, a big freeze went through the European olive groves a while back, killing them in great numbers. The specimens that survived were brought to Oregon as they proved adaptable to the cool, wet winters and hot, dry summers. Locally grown olives provide some of the fruit for the olive oil pressed on site. The rest comes from California during the olive harvest.

Mr. Hill arrived at the farm shop side of the Durant operation carrying a cello in a hard case. He had a no-nonsense strength about him, with both the solid build of an outdoorsman and the concentration of a serious cello player. He wore a plaid flannel shirt, habitual attire in the Pacific Northwest, the type of outfit someone working with wood might prefer.

Hill told me he grew up in Memphis and graduated with a degree in musical performance from the University of Tennessee at Chattanooga. He went on to perform as a freelance cellist, eventually moving into repair and making violins, violas, and cellos. It's surprising how many luthiers are not cello players, so Hill is quite the exception.

"When I was a little kid, I watched a PBS show about making string instruments. I asked my mom about this. Kept bringing it up until I got music lessons. They put me on the cello because of my size. Smaller kids got violins mostly," Hill explained.

We sat at a table under a people-heater in the olive oil tasting tent adjacent to the boutique farm market. The tent was open on one side, while the other sides blew around in the blustery, wet weather. Oregon spring temps are just warm enough to sit outside, if you're adventurous and want to get out of the house after several months of winter.

"You stuck with the cello, but aren't performing as much?" I asked.

"I didn't like auditioning. I could perform, but for grad school you audition, and for symphonies and groups, they want you to audition too," Hill recalled, leaning into the table. We received a short presentation about the different olive oil types and infused flavors including garlic and jalapeño from the Durant staff, then returned to our chairs to finish sampling the rest while we talked cello.

"How'd you move into making instruments?" I asked.

"A lot of repair goes on with string instruments. Most people don't know about all the things that go wrong—damage from dropping, strings breaking, all sorts of things. Simple fixes like rehairing a bow take time and expertise. Then there're cracks or something breaks," Hill said. When attending a music festival, he ran into a technician doing quick repairs. This luthier was working out of a practice room fixing all the instruments as they came in. Talking with him and watching him work grabbed Hill's interest.

From this starting point, Hill went on to attend the Violin Making School of America at age twenty-six. It is located in Salt Lake City, Utah, and was the most important school for these instruments in the country at the time. Since then, other schools have opened, including the famous Chicago School of Violin Making.

"I made violas in Atlanta after that. They're much faster to make. Cellos can take a year," Hill said. "The hours a luthier puts into it, cost of materials, the hours to make an instrument are brutal."

I asked him about the difference between making violins and violas.

"Violas have fewer rules. More freedom for expression. You can make different shapes. Be really creative," Hill explained. "Violins and cellos have some variation but largely conform to a set of norms."

The wind kept up the whole time, gusting around the open side of the tent where we were sitting. As weather changes from hot to cool, dry to damp, it affects a wooden instrument. I wondered how the cello Hill brought would be affected by the cold, wet afternoon. He stood his cello beside him, lifted the case, opened the front, and pulled out the instrument. The cello looked perfect, magnificent, and brand-new as the instrument was in the final stages of being built.

"All I have left to do on this instrument is age the appearance." Hill ran a hand over the front, feeling the smooth varnish.

I remembered learning about this when shopping for cellos that day.

He pulled a bow across the strings, scrutinizing whether the cello was in tune as he made adjustments. "Some musicians prefer to have the finish distressed so their cello looks antique. Furniture-makers do that for style. It's the same thing. You go into a furniture store and see new tables that have deliberately been beaten up to look a certain way."

I knew all this, but still, I have a hard time understanding the desirability of antiquing a brand-new cello made by a well-regarded luthier.

"It's up to the customer if I age a cello. About half the instruments are ordered this way. The rest I leave looking brand-new so they can age naturally," Hill said. "It's difficult to distress an instrument effectively. I add scrapes and gouges of different depths. Put in a small dent or chip with special tools. Takes a lot of time."

We talked about his workshop in his house. He explained he generally doesn't give tours since the space isn't set up for visitors.

"I'm still working on it," he told me.

A lot of luthiers work out of their house because of the convenience and cost savings. This is reminiscent of the luthiers of old, who often worked in a downstairs shop while living upstairs in the building.

"Would you like to hear my cello? I'll play it for you. Remember, it still needs a little finishing, but it's close to completion."

He played his cello right there in the open tent. We didn't ask anybody, he just started playing. All the tables were full with people chatting about olive oil and wine. To my surprise, even with the odd appearance of someone playing a cello out here, few heads turned.

Kile Hill played professionally, which he demonstrated by performing some classical selections on the spot from memory. The cello produced a rich, bright tone and sounded huge. That's no small compliment when playing outside with all the wind batting the tent around.

I'd made a reservation to take Hill over to the wine-tasting room. When the time arrived, he packed up the cello, and we walked in the spring gale through the nursery where two greenhouses contained plants for sale during warmer months.

At the wine-tasting room, we were greeted by the accommodating staff at the end of a long table made of thick Douglas fir with a live edge. Maybe all the wood used in buildings in the Pacific Northwest gives these places a relaxed feeling. In summer months, wine tasting is conducted outside, but in spring, being indoors with the doors closed and heat on is much more comfortable than the tent where we'd started.

Hill stood his cello at the end of the table so we could continue talking, while our wine steward poured the first smackerel of their chardonnay.

"Why did I start playing the cello at seventy-one? What caused me to start?" I asked Hill. Whenever I asked this question, I found it always stirred interest and different shades of responses from cello people, players, luthiers, and those who appreciate the instrument.

"You love music. Cello music is the most beautiful music of all time. Learning the cello is good for your brain. It's challenging, kicks your butt. It's aesthetically pleasing. You get creative playing."

"Good for your brain." I had heard that. Though from time to time, I'd heard that comic books inspired the imagination and learning a foreign language reorganized your mind, but that crossword puzzles weren't as good as tuning things up as is claimed. Music, especially making music with others, did a lot of good to keep thinking active. Everybody seemed to agree on that.

"Play some duets. That's even better for you. Get the *Béla Bartók Book of Duets, Volume One.* Find someone to play with," Hill said. Later that afternoon, I tracked down a cello duet version of "Ob-La-Di, Ob-La-Da" to play with another adult cello student of Mary Ann's at some point. I'd already found the music to "Here Comes the Sun" and was inching along learning that, so I figured duets were in my future for sure. I'd get there.

We'd tasted the second white wine by now. I looked forward to the reds, which I prefer. Oregon is known for pinot noir, and Durant has some personable vintages.

"If you're buying a cello, new or used, what do you think about?" I asked, as I was already thinking of my future self, and with the cost of these instruments, I would have to start saving for another, better model at the appropriate time. "What should someone look for?"

"Where it was made and when. Find out the name of the luthier, if that's available," Hill explained. "Was it taken care of? If people don't recognize the value of an instrument, it won't be stored properly, not usually."

That's why these instruments are tucked away in garages, basements, attics, and closets, and forgotten. Cellos are inherited, loaned out, given up on, and forgotten. That will lead to their decline.

"The spruce top on a cello is the most important wood. With bad spruce, you can't make a good cello," Hill said with a great deal of gusto.

Wood for the top of a Hill cello comes from Alaska. He orders in bulk, and the wood looks like firewood when it arrives. Hardwood, usually maple, is used for the backs and sides.

"The wood must be aged so it's dry and seasoned. Even if it's been kiln dried, I still store it for years to make sure it's thoroughly aged."

"I understand Stradivari formalized the size of a cello. Is that the one you make?" I asked.

Hill sipped a taste of the third pinot noir served by the tasting room staff, as he summed up a response to the word "Stradivari."

"There isn't a standard size, not exactly. The town of Cremona, Italy, had several instrument makers. Strad was one of them," he explained.

"Strad" refers to all things Stradivari—the man and family, and Stradivarius, the instruments he made. The Amati family and Guarneri family were big parts of the instrument-making brain trust in Cremona. Imagine an environment with so much quality innovation and interaction in one place. The early days of Silicon Valley come to mind as an innovation center, though it has devolved to be about vast sums of money in the hands of a few, an impossible real estate and housing situation, and a handful of peculiar personalities constantly in the news. I like to imagine Cremona might have struggled with these same pressures during the life of Antonio Stradivari with an ongoing storm of creativity and musical innovation in the air.

"Most luthiers build cellos based on an historic instrument. They duplicate it. I'm not a copyist. My cellos are a combination of different instruments. Successful cellos were also made in places other than Italy, Austria, and Germany. I take the best things from different instruments," Hill explained.

Inside the enclosed tasting room, the Kile Hill cello sounded even more robust and sweet as he played. The company of an accomplished cellist who also makes great cellos, playing in a winery tasting room, makes for a pleasant afternoon.

Jason Starkie—Luthier

Jason Starkie lives in Seattle, north of the University of Washington campus. His neighborhood looks a little more the way I'd expect Old Seattle was like, when the city seemed all about REI and less consumed by the ethos-changing Gates and Bezos gaddle-doodle. His modest house was built in the 1940s on an uphill slope, leaving space for a big front yard. Cozy and lived in, the design blends into the mash-up of young families and comfortable seniors. You'd never know high-quality cellos were crafted here as you drive by.

As with all the cello-makers I met, Starkie works out of his house. Or, more specifically, his narrow, single-car garage. When I pulled up, I double-checked the address, as there wasn't any outward indication this was where Starkie cellos dwelled.

The house sat above the street, requiring a climb up the path, then a scramble up steep exterior stairs to a narrow porch. Jason Starkie greeted me at the front door, then led me through his living room, where we descended two flights of interior stairs, all the way back down to street level to his garage workshop.

"Let me get a couple chairs."

Starkie slid two stools into the middle of the space. I positioned mine next to a joiner, where I could rest my paper tablet to take notes.

Jason Starkie is a tall, lanky fellow. He wore brown tweed pants, a black sweater, and a scarf reminiscent of what an Austin-Healey driver might wear to a car rally. A newsboy-style cap sat on Jason's head. His easygoing smile broadcast the sense he not only enjoyed the pace of his work but couldn't imagine doing anything else for a living.

His website has a similar artistic quality, with Starkie looking wistful in the landing page photo.

This luthier hadn't taken a formal route to making instruments. Instead of studying at an instrument-making school, Starkie attended San Francisco Art Institute. There, he met his friend and mentor Robert Brewer Young, who had established a significant reputation in stringed instruments.

Starkie usually makes a Strad Forma B instrument. "These are long and skinny" was how he described them. He also builds other models, such as a Rogeri design, which has a shorter string length preferred by players with smaller hands. His Grancino design offers a choice of maple, poplar, or willow back, and he says this design has almost the same dimensions as the Strad Forma B.

Starkie's studio has a less methodical air about it than I would have supposed. It's more artistic. He works with the same type of friendly clutter you expect to find in a painter's loft or sculptor's workshop. Though less organized than I would have imagined, I sensed he knew where he'd left each gewgaw, kickshaw, and bibelot a detail-oriented luthier may require. There was plenty of evidence of the cello-making process, especially sawdust and wood shavings swept in piles to the side. They flooded the space with the aroma of spruce and maple. A neck, back, and other pieces of instruments lay about in various stages of completion. Quarter-sawn wood rested like so many library books lined up on a shelf under a table, gradually waiting years to become properly seasoned, so they could take their turn to become a cello.

"Building instruments was hard for me to learn," Starkie said. "I had to understand how to recognize the corrections you need to make, as I couldn't see them at first. Now I easily recognize what I need to do to make a quality instrument."

The route he took to get from art school to becoming a luthier with his own brand took a couple loops into related crafts. He was a house carpenter for a long time before moving to making instruments.

"Combine art school training with carpentry, working with wood, and add New York City," he explained. "Creative people flock to New York. I did, and I started learning to make parts of instruments. I grew into making my own instruments from there and eventually moved back to Seattle to establish my own luthier business."

The instruments he makes are not identical. "A cello is your own voice, the voice of the musician," Starkie said. "I often adjust instruments for players so they get what they want from them."

I wondered what can be adjusted on a cello besides the strings. Do you have to take the instrument apart to rework a curve in the wood? What exactly can a luthier do to a finished cello?

Starkie explained that the major adjustment is the soundpost. This is the wooden dowel that stands up inside the cello as a brace between the top and back. I'd seen diagrams of this and figured the post was glued in place, unable to be adjusted. Starkie reached for an odd-shaped tool to demonstrate. He held out a long silver device with two bends in it—a soundpost adjuster for cellos. He showed how the adjuster inserts into the body of the instrument through the F-hole. The top and bottom of the soundpost can be nudged toward the middle or the outside.

He again emphasized how a cello is a living instrument that responds to weather, heat, cold, humidity. The post can be moved to tighten or loosen the tension within the body of the cello. Starkie demonstrated the way the tool could nudge the post. He showed me one of these posts, which appeared to be a simple dowel to fit the interior space.

"When a cellist attempts to adjust their sound post without the proper tools or training, they can knock the post loose, so it's rolling around inside. Then they bring it in," Starkie said. "I have to fish it out and use this cello soundpost inserter and remover to fix the problem."

Jason Starkie makes quality cellos.

Michael Doran—Luthier

Michael Doran lives in Duvall, a village just far enough outside of Seattle that gives the visitor a feeling of what a simpler life might be like, if you don't mind forgoing some conveniences. A rural highway runs through the middle of a knot of businesses there. Duvall is Doran's hometown.

His house is on a rise where he has his luthier workshop in another one-car garage. Garages have a substantial role in American industriousness. They've provided space for Henry Ford to build his first vehicle, Steve Jobs to start Apple, Disney his first movies, Amazon and so many other companies to get going. These days, one-car garages seem uniquely suited to cello making.

Doran is a compact fellow in jeans and a long-sleeve sweater with his dark hair tied back, his beard reminding me of a rock climber or someone who spends weekends canoeing. Duvall is close to the Cascades foothills, so he fits right in with the terrain.

"Let me show you around." Doran guided me through his front door. We took a hard left through his living room into the connected, single-car garage.

At first, his neatly arranged workshop seemed small, neatly arranged with little going on, until he got into the details of what's involved in making beautiful, resonant cellos from scratch. This first impression came from the space being well-organized and practically spotless.

The business of cutting and shaping wood produces a lot of shavings, sawdust, and other debris. However, the floor was spic-and-span, to the point of appearing disinfected, like you could eat off it. A big blue tub brimmed with wide, blond, curled wood shavings that rested quietly by the door near a shop-vac. Doran mentioned tidying up before I came over, though I sensed he approached cello making methodically, so having a clean, well-lit space suited his work style.

Along all the walls, Doran stored tools and supplies, including peculiar glue jars. Pieces of ordinary lumber, scraps that looked like so much firewood, rested in racks where they could gracefully age, waiting their turn to be fashioned into cellos.

Before we got into more specifics about his work, I asked him the question that led me to track him down in the first place. "What motivated me to pursue the cello out of the blue?"

"The cello is a beautiful, seductive instrument," Doran explained. "I love to listen to the cello, but I don't play it. An interest in woodworking got me into making instruments. That, and playing the mandolin. I'm a mandolin player."

Michael Doran told me he attended a high school focused on nature and the arts. The activity that interested him most was making archery bows. Archery bow construction involves bending and tapering wood. He got into exploring different designs and construction methods to make these. From there, an interest in bluegrass music prompted him to make a mandolin. He made three before producing one that could actually be played. With that success, he moved to trying to make a violin.

Doran explained how he headed to the local library where he found a book titled *Violin Making for the Amateur*.

"It was a lousy book for learning to make a violin. It really only showed how to make VSO: violin-shaped objects," Doran said.

As his interest grew, he headed to the Violin Making School of America in Salt Lake City, where he worked all day learning to make violins and cellos, while working all night to pay the rent. At the school, Doran made ten instruments: eight violins, a viola, and a cello. Violins were faster to make, but he found cellos more satisfying.

"Isn't the Stradivari Forma B cello the standard for cellos?" At this point I still thought this was a simple truth about cellos. However, the look on Doran's face suggested I suffered another major misconception about how much cello luthiers agreed on anything.

"No, the Strad B does not have a great bass," Doran said, setting me straight.

"Did you bring forth a new cello design?" I realized I was creating some sort of birth myth, but I imagined Doran experimenting with shapes and sizes in his shop until he made the ideal cello.

"No, some luthiers do that," he said.

"What's your approach?" I asked.

He explained he mostly makes a cello fashioned after those created by Giuseppe Giovanni Battista Guarneri and, just to confuse things, was known as *Joseph Guarnerius filius Andreae*. He was the second son of Andrea Guarneri, thus filius Andrea. The Guarneri Family of violin makers lived and worked in Cremona, Italy. It is easy to get the many members of this family confused, as the whole bunch of them were luthiers who produced outstanding instruments.

The particular cello Doran makes was created in 1697 and at one time, was in the possession of the Royal Academy of Music, known as RAM, in London. It is currently in private hands and represented by Tarisio, an international company that conducts auctions and private sales of some three thousand fine instruments and bows annually.

Doran feels the filius Andrea design, as he refers to the cello he makes, has a deeper bass than the Stradivarius Forma B. He builds this model from drawings made directly from measurements of the cello during its stay in the RAM collection. Luthiers gained additional information about the woods and glues and varnishes and, perhaps, the Italian soul of this masterpiece during their examination. What is the difference between this cello from Guarneri and a Stradivari? These and other famous cello makers knew each other well and worked down the street from each other.

In their excellent book *Antonio Stradivari, His Life and Work*, authors W. Henry, Arthur F., and Alfred E. Hill make a point about this, saying, "It is, for instance, known to not a few that Stradivari violins give forth a character of tone perfectly distinct from those of his great rival, Giuseppe Guarneri 'del Gesù.' Why? The answer to the question is not to be found in the construction alone, as there exist Guarneris and Stradivaris built practically upon the same lines, yet each retains its own quality of tone." In other words, it remains a mystery.

RAM allows the instruments in its collection to be examined and measured so they can be recreated, with the hope that sharing this information will support the development of better instruments. Other great museums are typically willing to do the same thing.

The original Guarneri instrument Doran builds a version of was roughly valued at this moment between $1.5 and $2 million according to a Tarisio representative I recently spoke with—though prices move with the market. Cellos of this quality with the Guarnerius lineage will typically appreciate at about 4 percent annually. Some investors will purchase an instrument like this and simply hang on to it until the market is right to sell. They also might lend the instrument to a professional cellist to perform on or eventually donate it to a museum.

Out of all the cellos Doran could have picked, how did he land on this one? He explained that he met a cello maker from England, Robin Aitchison, who used to work for RAM as their resident luthier taking care of the instruments. Aitchison had extensive access and information on the cellos in the collection, and this was one of the first models he started making.

Doran met Aitchison when he was instructing at the Oberlin Violin Makers Workshop where they made a copy of this cello together.

"I liked the reproduction and was looking for a new model. The thing that really sold me on the instrument and got me to try it is the size. Old cellos are often too big, and then they can get cut down to be made smaller—which is a whole story itself," Doran recalled.

But this one was made in what he considered to be a good size by modern standards and was left untouched. He tried the cello and felt like it worked well right off the bat and has made minor adjustments and improved on his design since.

For the front of his cellos, Doran uses Engelmann spruce from Northern British Columbia. The wood has a fine, even texture and a consistently straight grain. He finds bigleaf maple too soft for the backs and sides. The other species of American maple—sugar maple, red maple, silver maple, and others—tend to be too hard. Instead, he uses maple from Europe because the species have that middle density he's looking for. Some makers do use American maple, both bigleaf and others, but Doran says the grain looks different, and he finds he can pick them out from across the room—which is fine, but not his preference.

He showed me samples of this wood in his shop, holding out rough, thick slabs with nothing distinctive to separate these samples from any old pile of wood stacked up next to a campfire ring. They could have been so much kindling if not carefully stored to age in a luthier's shop. That said, the more I visit cello makers and see this raw wood, the better I am at understanding what their tone wood looks like when it is delivered to them and that it's quality wood yet to be shaped into a quality instrument.

Doran pointed out the differences in the grain on these samples.

"Some makers use willow or poplar for the backs. This gives a softer, warmer, more colorful sound, but maple provides more power and projection. I feel I can soften the sound of the maple back, so I stick with it unless there's a request for a different wood."

Michael Doran makes three or four cellos a year. Only forty years old, he'd already made seventy-six instruments when I met him: forty cellos, five violas, and the rest violins, with more to come.

We went around the shop studying the tools he used. The most impressive were the tiny hand planers. These shave off ultra-thin ribbons of wood to thin and shape it.

"Look at what these can do." Doran opened a drawer, retrieved a box, and lifted the lid to display inch-long and smaller planers, including quarter-of-an-inch planers the size of a thumbnail. He selected a particularly small one and demonstrated how the tool worked on a cello top. The micro-planer accurately shaved a diaphanous slice off the surface. A thin, thin, thin tissue of wood.

The great delights of Doran's studio were his large, extraordinary Wizard of Oz-style antediluvian power tools. They make quite an impression. These are Delta tools and have cast-iron bases. Their weight lowers the center of gravity and reduces vibration. He makes cellos using a 1936 band saw. His drill press is from 1942, the year his dad was born. A 1946 band saw dates to the year his mother was born. His newest tool is a 1968 router. Historic Delta tools even have cool, timeless art deco styling.

"I bought these at scrap prices and refurbished them," Doran said.

They are large, floor-mounted American-made power tools by Delta Machinery in Milwaukee, Wisconsin. Same town where Harley-Davidson famously originated. Milwaukee is proudly a working-class city with a strong tradition for design and manufacturing.

Doran went on about his Delta tools. "Those are all my machines! I really fell in love with the beauty of the industrial design from back when things were made well. Machines like this are so sturdy that you can hardly kill them. Comparable modern machines of similar accuracy exist, but I'd pay at least ten times more for them. Plus, I get a lot of enjoyment from tinkering with this equipment. I've never wanted or needed to hide my machines away in another room—I like looking at them!"

Doran also built his own workbench with a thick, raw wood top and legs. It is fabulously solid and weighs four hundred pounds. He opened a cabinet to show me a tailpiece. This is the ebony wood that holds the strings at the bottom of the cello front. They are often made of plastic these days. The version he uses is made in France. He feels the tailpiece has more influence on a cello than the violin.

"One last thing is the endpin." He rolled open a piece of muslin with narrow pockets to reveal a quiver of endpins made from different materials. A couple were carbon fiber. These were tech black and weighed nothing. The endpin is another way persnickety cellists will customize their cellos.

"The carbon fiber is really popular on a new cello." Doran took out one endpin after another from his bundle so I could examine them. Steel is most often used for endpins and is considered traditional. There are also some endpins from Japan made of brass and filled with different types of material. These uber-custom end rods can run into big money, with some costing over one thousand dollars.

We spent a lot of time looking at a cello body that was close to being finished. This portion of the instrument in this state was unfinished and the wood raw. He still needed to add the neck and many other bits and pieces before completing the finish. Doran seldom has a finished cello in his studio for someone to play. I wished he kept a few around to listen to and get a feel for his instruments, but they are sent to the buyer after completion, so there were none.

I was mesmerized by his organization, the pride he showed in his tools, and the instruments he produced. I wondered what a Michael

Doran cello would sound like and wanted to play this one when he finished it.

"You can check out the cello I'm working on when it's finished. I usually play it in for a week or two after it's done to get the wood working together, make any adjustments that are needed. I might adjust the sound peg, hot rod it a little," he explained. "It's hard to know when I'll be completing a cello. You just keep working on it until suddenly it's done. But I'll let you know."

We arranged to keep in touch through the building process so when he reached the finish line, I could come up to Seattle and play a brand-new Doran cello.

It was a couple months before Doran let me know I could try out his new Guarnerius model cello. I had just ten days to get up to Seattle before he shipped his just-finished cello to its new owner.

I bought an Amtrak ticket to ride up to see it, but when a landslide closed the tracks, I dug up some frequent flyer miles and flew to Sea-Tac, then took Seattle light rail into the city. From the station, I walked three blocks to the Seattle Public Library, where Doran had reserved a music practice room.

Rem Koolhaas, a Dutch architect known for new modernism design, created the main Seattle Public Library, which opened in 2004. Many people had encouraged me to visit this undulating structure, as there has been a lot of noise about its out-of-the-ordinary design. The library's skin juts out at odd angles—not in the square shape of a typical skyscraper. Instead, the building appeared to have been folded, then partially unfolded. Its off-kilter appearance was a prominent feature on the Seattle skyline.

I arrived early enough to be on time, though finding the rehearsal room we'd reserved turned into an obstacle course, as navigating the place is no easy matter. The interior space, the architect claimed, aimed at sweeping the library into the digital age. Floors spiral around so you can't figure out where you are or where you're going. Others get cut off in midair. The library isn't helped by being one of the principal buildings in the neighborhood with public restrooms, which attracts a lot of folks for only that reason. There is something just wrong about the layout of the place.

Architecture critic Lawrence Cheek wrote in a 2007 *Seattle Post-Intelligencer* piece that he found the building "confusing, impersonal, uncomfortable, and oppressive," In addition to being "decidedly unpleasant, relentlessly monotonous, with cheesy detail." I found the space so screwed up inside that finding anything seemed unachievable, leaving me yearning for the dull miles of shelving in old, warehouse-style stacks. Books were so easy to find in those places.

After a lengthy search, I located the right librarian to take me to the rehearsal room.

Once ensconced in the room, his cello immediately sprang from the graphite case. He glowed like a kid bursting with pride, showing a friend "Look what I built."

I pulled the bow across the strings, creating an immersive sound. Each note sounded clean and clear with a woody depth, delivering a fulfilling, rich tone. Doran had added what passed for wear patterns on the new cello to give it an aged look. Studying a brand-spanking-new cello that could pass, at a distance, for a decades-old instrument is disquieting.

Once Doran shipped this cello to a music store in Boston, he shared the text response he received from the music shop he made it for:

> Your cello is a huge hit. I am not surprised, but I can say in all honesty that it is rare to find an instrument that has such universal appeal around here. We, by design, seek out players with different tastes and approaches to sound, and then there is our workshop, and then me. Everyone looking for different things in an instrument. So far, everyone loves your cello. Bravo. VERY nice work. The sound is prominent, interesting, easy to shape, ample support and clarity on the bottom, and the top sings. The cello is loud, but in no way brassy or offensive. And the response is such that it can be played softer and sweetly as needed by a sensitive player.
>
> It is truly rewarding for me to be in the position to provide such a positive report. I do not get to write emails like this often enough. Thank you for sending your cello here—it will do well.
>
> Please send me an invoice at your convenience. And keep us in mind for another cello in the future. I do not expect to have this long, unless we can't stand to let it go!

I believe that in three hundred years, cellists will seek out Michael Doran cellos the way cellos by Stradivari and Guarneri and Amani and other noted luthiers are today.

Chapter 15
The Cellists

Having explored the workshops of regional luthiers, I asked Port-land Cello Project, Artistic Director Douglas Jenkins, for suggestions for professional cello players to talk with—especially someone taking an unusual approach.

"Talk with Gideon Freudmann," came the response.

Jenkins provided links to Freudmann's website, and from there I found his TED Talk, along with other resources, including a list of upcoming performances and an introduction to CelloBop. Hadn't heard that one before. CelloBop is the name he gave his style of composition and performance.

His website provided links to videos with his music that are fun to watch. His style is described as an improvisational blend of classical, blues, jazz, electronic, funk, and folk. He is a founding member of the Portland Cello Project, where he continues be a contributing composer.

I tracked down Gideon to discuss the cello. I was surprised to learn he didn't live in Portland anymore, but had moved to Whidbey Island, north of Seattle, a short ferry ride from the mainland. Island living allows him all the nearby amenities of a global urban hub while avoiding a lot of big-city hassles, and snagging breezy views of orcas making their way around Puget Sound.

Susan and I drove up on a weekend adventure to meet Gideon on his island on an early spring day. His house was light and airy with a living room full of arty knickknacks and towering white bookshelves, with a peekaboo view of the ocean out the back.

Gideon is wiry and energetic, a maverick cellist with the dash of eccentricity I'd been searching for. His music studio fills a room some people might use as a ground-floor office. The studio has a thick, ornate rug covering much of the floor to dampen stray sounds when recording. The cello he uses most of the time resides on a stand. There's a modest amount of electronics for recording and layering music, creating a sound as if several cellos are playing together. He occasionally sings too, so there's a microphone for that.

A few steps beyond the studio the living room opened onto picture windows.

"Have a seat." He indicated a couch, while he took the chair across the room.

He brought his cello along to play examples of his signature Cello-Bop and other musical styles as we talked about them. We launched into a range of cello topics: how I was just beginning to play the instrument, the way he provides music for silent films, and some music theory explaining what draws people like me to the cello.

"I'm a new cello player. I still squeak a lot," I said.

"Embrace the squeaky sounds." Gideon sat in an upholstered chair before a wall with built-in shelving. I recognized this spot from some short videos he'd posted in which he played some of his compositions.

"I don't squeak as much as I did when I started," I said. "You started playing when you were eight. How did you pick the cello?"

Gideon explained that he liked the way the cello looks and sounds. He couldn't imagine standing on stage with a flute or having confidence with a violin.

"My back hurts just thinking about holding a violin with my arms up in the air like that, the sound right next to my ear. With a cello, the sound come out the front, projects—fills the room."

"The cello's more comfortable to play than a lot of instruments," I said.

"On stage, there is something there because the cello's right in front of you. A cello's responsive. It rests on your sternum. You feel the vibrations in your skeleton."

He went on to explain how classical cello players use a bow to play most of the time. How they're also taught to pluck strings in a formal manner, which requires plucking directly out from the string. Gideon demonstrated the informality of his method, a far more relaxed approach to plucking, that involves thunking the strings sideways, the way a bass player does. He also creates chords and strums the cello the way guitar players do while holding the cello in an upright position, whereas a guitar is held sideways.

He explained how he's been experimenting with these techniques since he started, playing some examples as he explained. "Adding a seventh makes the chord sound more lounge-y. Adding a ninth is fancy or jazzy, depending on how it fits into what you're playing. You can animate the chord with a climbing baseline," which he played, enlivening the sound as if it started walking around on its own.

Guitar playing seemed directly related to how this CelloBop style is performed. However, Gideon denoted many differences, all obvious once pointed out.

"On the cello, the strings are farther apart than on the guitar. The fingerboard is curved on the cello, while flat and fretted on the guitar. The rounded fingerboard helps you clear an adjacent string and use the pad of your fingers. Also, a guitar has six strings, and you have four fingers."

Remember, cellists don't count the thumb as a finger.

"Guitar tuning is different. It's tuned in fourths, except for B, which is a third. The top and bottom strings are both tuned in E, which delivers a natural resonance."

Gideon went on to demonstrate how he shapes chords by putting the third on top to produce variations in their sound. To better show us how he layered sound, we moved into his studio so he could use his electronics. He took a seat facing several effects pedals. They were each about the size of a deck of cards and lined up in a row on the floor. He tapped one with his foot to lay down a baseline, and looped the sound so it played continuously. He laid down another musical line over that, making it sound as though two extra musicians were in the room. He went on to play over these while they repeated. It was mesmerizing.

"How many layers of sound can you have going at one time?" I asked.

"It's like a painter laying down coats of paint. The painting doesn't necessarily get better because there are more layers." To demonstrate, Gideon added another layer, which competed with what he had going and muddled the individual musical lines.

You've probably heard Gideon Freudmann's compositions, his playing, and even a little of him singing, whether you know it or not. His work appeared in the TV series *Weeds*. Look at the first episode in Season 3, for the scene where a kid gets ahold of a car and starts circling it around a parking lot. The lyric is "I drive an American car."

His music appears in commercials for Apple, Chrysler, and other companies, as well as movies, including the animated short *Denmark*, produced by the Portland Cello Project. His music is in the background during a quick scene in the Jane Fonda and Lily Tomlin movie *Moving On*. Soon after I learned this, I was on a flight to Europe watching that film and heard Gideon's music while over Greenland. Lily Tomlin is on her way to kill someone while Gideon's composition fortifies the action.

Gideon also provides live accompaniment for silent films. Buster Keaton films are a frequent request for him to add music to.

"I am accompanying *The General* at the Myrna Loy Theater in Helena, Montana, in a couple weeks," he said. "To prepare, I watch the film several times. Then I watch it a couple times fast. This helps to better understand the overall flow of the story."

"Any tips for an old guy determined to play the cello?" I asked.

"What do you have the most trouble with?" he asked.

"Almost everything." I considered providing a list of things but stuck with two. "Accidently playing two strings at the same time is one. Another is finding the right spot to put my fingers to hit the note."

Gideon nodded. "Common problems. Pull the bow straight across the strings. It's easy to make the mistake of lifting as you pull across." He demonstrated how keeping your elbow straight out to the side helps with this. "Also, playing two strings at once helps you concentrate on keeping the bow perpendicular to the strings."

He showed how holding the bow at an angle as it crosses the strings changes the sound. The bow hairs are no longer aligned, and you can hear the change for the worse.

"For learning where to place your fingers on the fingerboard, don't put tape or a dot on top. Put a small piece of tape on the side for the first and fourth positions. That way you can either feel where the tape is or glance over to see it." Gideon showed where the tape reminder would go. "Eventually, you get a feel for it, and it comes naturally."

I tried that. Placed a narrow strip of blue painter's tape on the side of my cello's fingerboard. That helps a beginner because you can feel with your thumb where it is. When I took it off months later, my teacher described it as, "Taking off the training wheels."

Cello at a Salon

Soon after our meeting with Gideon, word reached me that I could listen to CelloBop, an entire little concert, played during a salon in someone's front room down where I live. I let Abbie, the host, know Susan and I were coming. I'd never been to a salon before and thought they were something you did in Paris with Gertrude Stein and the Moderns back in the day. The idea that people participated in this sort of soiree intrigued me, if just to find out how weird it would be to sit in someone's front room listening to a professional cello performance.

Historically, a salon involves a social, or intellectual, or otherwise artistic gathering where discussions center on a single topic. A salon might display art with the artist in attendance, a writer could read from their work, a musician or small ensemble might play for the gathering of the compatibly minded.

Susan and I weren't sure what to expect when we arrived on an unusually warm May evening. The days were starting to lengthen, and winds brought hot, dry air to a city more accustomed to a cool, damp overcast.

Abbie's house sat in an older section of Portland, east of downtown, a neighborhood lush with mature trees and overgrown laurels pushing onto the sidewalk.

We were guided into the narrow entryway to find a man seated in a chair before what looked like a child's cash register. It was a toy but worked well enough to keep track of totals and had a real drawer to store full-size bills. The recommended donation was twenty to twenty-five dollars per person. This was a bargain, since the suggested amount was a fraction of the cost of a ticket in a theater.

The salon began with an informal potluck spread across the kitchen table. Guests were invited to arrive an hour before the show, chitchat with fellow salonists and nibble on chocolate chip cookies and potato chips. We brought a chilled bottle of white wine, which disappeared into a picnic cooler on the kitchen floor.

Gideon would play in Abbie's long living room, which she'd filled with several rows of folding chairs with hard, flat seats. A better bet for comfort would have been the overstuffed couch turned sideways to the room. It looked soft and had cushions. We should have snagged a spot there but failed. Abbie told me that the six-inch-high stage was meant to be temporary, but since they were organizing so many of these salons, they just left it at the end of their living room.

Gideon drove up to Portland from Crescent City, California that morning, having given a concert the day before. After six hours behind the steering wheel, he still seemed perky, hanging out with the audience in the kitchen for half an hour before mentioning it was time to start. A couple quick minutes later, Abbie stepped to the stage to introduce Gideon, who kicked into gear.

There is unfathomable joy in sitting near a good cello player as they perform. I experienced the same glad response from listening up close as I had at the lecture while on the Camino. In Spain, our lecturer had played live to a similarly sized audience where we could sit up front. This helped me understand why people respond to the sound of wooden stringed instruments. The experience is warm and delicious, especially when you're right there in front of the cellist.

What would it have been like to have been in such a room listening to a cello concert in the era of Stradivarius, Ruggieri, Amati, Guarneri, and similarly gifted luthiers, with the innovations they were making in these instruments? The audience must have listened for qualities in the rich woodiness and compared their creations, trying to come up with ways to produce an even more penetrating, emotional sound. Imagine the conversations they had about the curve of a cello's arched top or how the size of the instrument fit a player's hands. The quality of the varnish. How intense would their competition have been? To what extent did they share discoveries about creating these instruments—or attempt to disguise them from the competition?

Gideon often plays solo gigs or adds one or two other musicians to perform. When I asked him what he likes about playing this way, he contrasted salon performances to a cellist performing as part of a symphony, where there are many constraints. For example, the symphony has the power of so many musicians together. But all the instruments have to have their bows moving in the same direction. If you are bowing opposite everyone else, it doesn't look right. In a symphony, you can also stop playing and no one would notice.

Gideon did play a little classical music, the first *Bach Cello Concerto*, referring to it as "an old chestnut." He played this piece with expression, though his passion lay in performing his own compositions. You could hear the joy in them. Some of these included lyrics he wrote, and he sang those with a straightforward resolve. He dug into the "James Bond Theme" too. Laid down the famous Bond three-note bassline, then layered the familiar strains of 007 onto that. He said he played the Bond theme for a friend once. She didn't recognize it and asked if this was a new tune he wrote.

Gretchen Yanover

Gretchen Yanover has the best posture.

When she's playing the cello, she sits upright in what appears to be a yoga pose. I listened to part of a two-hour session where she projected energy and focus as she presented her compositions.

Gretchen performed in the lobby of a contemporary Seattle office building over a lunch hour. I took Amtrak up from Portland and walked over from the station.

Once I determined what part of the block-spanning building I should enter, I wandered the maze of mysteriously arranged corridors until I caught a few notes from a distant cello and honed in on the music. I finally came around a bend in all the gray space where corridors kink and converge, to find Gretchen playing an electronic cello. I took a seat upfront, on one of the round, heavily cushioned chairs.

My discovery of Gretchen Yanover came when I searched for cellists and found her TED Talk fascinating. The talk highlighted her playing and discussing some background. Notably, the talk opens with Gretchen performing on electric cello barefoot, wearing a summery dress. We see cello players in formal black symphony attire most of the time, so watching and listening to a contemporary cellist looking breezy and stylish is arresting.

She talked about discovering the cello at a Seattle public school in sixth grade, and immediately being drawn to the instrument. Gretchen explained her mother is Black, but quoted her mom saying, "Don't call me anything other than human." Her father is Jewish, but she said, "He assured me that is not white."

Gretchen earned a BA in music performance from the University of Washington, then went on to teach and perform. Using the loop pedal transformed her work, propelling her to improvise and compose more. She has recorded several albums.

Trying to categorize her music gave me a lot of trouble, which is a good thing, since so many musicians are quickly cornered when we label them. I asked Gretchen how she described her own compositions and playing style. She responded, "Well, I have some descriptions by other folks."

> With an electric cello in hand and a loop pedal underfoot, Yanover is her own one-woman band. Playing and layering her melodies, she crafts instrumental atmospheres that grow and transform onstage.
> —Maggie Molloy, *NPR Slingshot*

> Seattle cellist Gretchen Yanover combines her classical chops and gorgeous tone with layered electronic loops to create a stunning hybrid of minimalism and romanticism.
> —Steve Peters, Jack Straw Cultural Center

Gretchen's elegant compositions are less about a melody line and more about a pattern of musical thought, making them fascinating to listen to. When we talked about different cellos, Gretchen explained that plenty of great cellists aren't playing expensive cellos. They could be playing the cello they started with years ago and think it sounds fine. She uses her traditional wooden cello for symphony or ensemble performances, but prefers the lightweight amplified electronic cello for solo gigs.

In addition to lunchtime in downtown lobbies, she plays in casual environments. Not in noisy restaurants, but in senior centers or with events at the airport where it's "wallpaper music and you can listen to it in all different ways."

One story stood out. Gretchen's schoolteacher told her parents that she felt Gretchen clearly had a talent for the cello and they should look into getting her private lessons. They found a teacher. During the first lesson, Gretchen said she explained how excited she was about playing, even asking specifically to play Bach.

In response, the teacher replied, "Oh, you'll never be able to play that."

She told her parents this, and they wisely found her another teacher.

Hearing cellists like Gretchen perform expands the understanding of what kinds of music a cello can play, well beyond the traditional classical repertoire.

As we were wrapping up our conversation, I asked, "Do you have any tips for me about learning to play?"

Gretchen replied, "Yes, get a mirror. Practice in front of it to check your technique."

I laughed and explained she was at least the fourth person to tell me to get a mirror.

"I'm not surprised," Gretchen said. "It's a common tool for learning."

Charlotte Moorman, Avant-Garde Cellist

One cellist I wish I'd met is a thought-provoking performance artist who deserves more fame. Charlotte Moorman was born in Arkansas in 1933. Moorman started the cello at age ten, going on to earn one MA from the University of Texas and another in cello performance from The Julliard School. She established herself as a classical concert cellist with the American Symphony Orchestra in New York but grew tired of the routine. With the influence of the lively New York City performance art scene in the 1960s, she moved into the avant-garde arena.

For a time, her roommate, Yoko Ono, helped fuel Moorman's artistic evolution, helping make connections to a variety of artists. A frequent collaborator she worked with was Korean American Nam June Paik, a video art pioneer.

Moorman kept the cello at the center of her work, even adding the eye-catching novelty of performing playing topless or just plain nude. She was arrested for indecent exposure during one concert, causing her to miss playing all the movements of her piece. The charges were later dropped. She performed similarly unattired shows in Europe without any fuss.

She tweaked her shows, adding variations. In one, she wrapped up in a plastic sheet, nude underneath, of course, to perform on her instrument. During a mind-bending collaboration with Paik, called "TV Bra for Living Sculpture," a pair of mini-TVs were positioned on her top as she played the cello. In another show, a cello was frozen in a block of ice, which she managed to play in a chilly state of undress.

Charlotte Moorman burbled with chaotic energy as she challenged norms of cello playing.

My Teacher—Mary Ann Coggins Kaza

Mary Ann had many violin teachers as her abilities improved. One of them, a Mr. Creitz, would stomp on her feet to get her to keep time. "Back then, it was all about discipline," she remembered. Her teachers had her repeat scales and arpeggios relentlessly.

She was accepted into the Portland Youth Philharmonic and attended Tanglewood youth programs twice, where she met Leonard Bernstein and violin teacher Louis Krasner. Another teacher, Raphael Spiro, encouraged learning different styles, including jazz, pop, and improv.

During this learning process, she recognized she was an orchestral violinist, not a soloist. To augment income from playing, Mary Ann worked at the biggest department store in Portland at the time, Meier Frank, in their basement restaurant. Over time, she moved to the nicer upper floor restaurant, sometimes playing her violin for diners. During this sojourn, Mary Ann completed a degree at Portland State University in musical performance on violin with her second instrument, the cello, all while playing the violin evenings wherever she could.

Eventually, she became a runner in the Meier Frank executive suites before advancing to administrative assistant. From there, she moved on to become the company's safety director. "Working there helped support me playing the violin with the Oregon Symphony for forty-four years," she told me. Early on, a symphony violinist earned all of two thousand dollars a year—hardly enough to stay afloat. For twenty years, she worked both jobs and even rose to the position of the orchestra's personnel manager, demonstrating a lot of determination to live a musician's life.

In time, Mary Ann became the third wife of a fellow musician and conductor, Eugene Kaza, who had six children. They had a twenty-five-year age difference.

The story goes that Eugene's pregnant mother was attending a Ringling Bros. and Barnum & Bailey Circus performance when the bleachers collapsed, causing his premature birth. Eugene was a former Oregon Symphony violinist and also a music teacher at a local high school. Altogether, he became a major influence on Portland's young musicians as a conductor and mentor to Portland Youth Philharmonic players.

Mary Ann's husband had a number of medical problems, and at one point, doctors gave him only two months to live—he went on living another twenty years. Adding to the complications, her husband moved to a facility where he could be cared for. To accommodate this situation, she lived in a Motel 6 just down the freeway. This proved to be a reasonably priced environment, as the unit had a kitchen and would allow her to keep her six dachshunds. She visited her husband every day while working and playing the violin and caring for her many dogs.

Motel 6 told Mary Ann she held the record for the longest stay of any of their guests anywhere. When the CEO came out to visit this hotel, he'd even take her out to dinner. She stayed there sixteen years until the Covid pandemic temporarily closed the place and she had to find an apartment to move into.

Mary Ann had a lot of violin teachers when learning to play. Too many of them focused on discipline, repetition, and authority. "I never let that teaching style break my spirit," she said.

Now that she's in a regular apartment, she admits, "I'm a hoarder. Well, actually I'm a collector." She counted off owning five cellos, two ukuleles, five violas, probably a dozen violins, an antique drum set, clarinets, bassoons, and a bass clarinet. There's also an upright piano and a baby grand she bought when she had a big slot machine win at a local casino. She keeps a ukulele in the car to play when a train stops traffic so she has something to do.

Over the years, Mary Ann has played with many groups, including the Oregon Ballet, Portland Opera, Raphael Spiro Quartet, and community orchestras.

Chapter 16
A Mirror

Jenelle Steele at the violin store, Mary Ann, Gideon Freudmann, Gretchen Yanover with perfect posture, and even Kenneth Slowik at the Smithsonian recommended I practice while looking into a mirror, so it was time to go find one.

Jenelle repairs instruments and bows at David Kerr Violin Shop and was the first to mention practicing in front of a mirror. "I'm a cello player too. A mirror helps a lot. You can see what you're really doing, not just what you think you're doing," Jenelle explained.

Kenneth Slowik mentioned a mirror during our surprise conversation. "A mirror will help you; it's really a good idea. You will catch your mistakes," he told me on the phone.

Gideon Freudmann recommended getting a mirror too. "It really helps seeing the alignment of the bow to keep it perpendicular to the strings. Also, for bow placement, keeping the bow in the sweet spot between the bottom of the fingerboard and the bridge."

A few mirrors on Craigslist looked like interesting possibilities. I eliminated all the overpriced options; about half fell into that category. Other mirrors were too decorative, including some with eagles on top. Or they were old grandma mirrors—cheap and ornate and dusty. A couple big mirrors looked interesting, but how would I move them around?

Susan cautioned that whatever I picked out would need to fit our décor, such as it is. We don't have a recognizable interior design scheme, I pointed out. The living room walls are mostly white, at least in the small area where I practice my cello, there's not a lot to work with, so design-wise there weren't a lot of restrictions.

A mirror of interest was priced well with an appealing size. But it was in Sandy, a small town up the hill toward Mount Hood, way out in the country. An email exchange ensued. The owner was willing to reduce his price. Then he said he'd deliver the mirror for an additional twenty-five dollars. He was "making some firewood deliveries down there in the next couple days."

Another choice, from the Brooklyn Furniture Mall, was designed in a Craftsman style with a square base and rectangular mirror, and could easily tilt and be reoriented.

Brooklyn is a Portland neighborhood with a bunch of railroad tracks and peripheral businesses. When I arrived, I found the furniture mall to be a large space full of nicer-than-usual used dressers, tables, and chairs. The Craftsman mirror turned out to be a fifteen-year-old piece, made in China, using wood veneer. Narrow strips of wood created decorative lattice elements in the style of windows, which narrowed the width of the reflections.

"I need to sit down to see if it works. I'm going to be watching myself play the cello," I said.

The woman running this section of furniture pulled over a chair for me. I sat admiring myself for a long time, tilting the mirror to different degrees, imagining how the setup would work with the cello. She readily came down on the cost when I asked, "What's your bottom line?"

Now, when people come into the living room, they see the back of the mirror. Some cello quotes are stuck on the back, along with an "I Love Cello" sticker. I've hung drawings of cellos that look like old magazine cover art, abstract cello paintings, and Man Ray's woman-as-cello picture.

They say a cello sounds like a human voice. Better than that, it reminded me of the art of Man Ray, who turned a woman into a cello.

Man Ray was an avant-garde artist in 1920s Paris who drew two cello F-holes, that you see on the front of a cello, on his girlfriend's back and photographed her. He called the photo "violin," but she's definitely a cello in the picture. Way too big to be a violin. She wore only a turban in the shot, with her head turned to the side. The result was a simple, clever image suggesting a cello.

The girlfriend's name was Kiki de Montparnasse, which is the kind of name you'd expect a model to have in the 1920s who was doing this sort of modeling work. The original photograph of her creating the ageless cello motif has since sold for over twelve million dollars at auction.

Chapter 17
King of the Surf Guitar

There were other musicians I became interested in and met over the years. Some shaped how I experience music. Some I grew up with.

My first car had an AM radio. Several stations played Top 40 songs and talked up all the hoopla around new bands, hot singers, punchy tunes with new rhythms. Just what a kid growing up in Southern California needed to make sense of things—as much as it's possible to make sense of things down there.

The band I most identified with at the time was the Beach Boys. They shot the photos for their groundbreaking *Pet Sounds* album at the San Diego Zoo. This album—considered to be one of the most influential albums in music—was released in 1966, three years before I had a job selling cheeseburgers at the world-famous zoo's Safari Kitchen. This gave me a weird connection to the Beach Boys, or, at least it did in my distorted teenage way of thinking.

I have seen the iconic group perform live many times. The audience always sings along with them, creating an atmosphere that's just plain joyous, the way a high school reunion triggers singing the school's anthem. The vocal performance getting a little more ragged every time they get together.

Another big name in surf music was Richard Anthony Monsour. He was born in 1937 and grew up in Massachusetts, where he started out in cowboy music, getting tagged with the stage name Dick Dale by a fellow musician.

Dale moved to Los Angeles in high school when his father took an aircraft industry job there. He was part Lebanese and grew up playing Middle Eastern music. He incorporated this into his guitar playing. Interestingly, he played his right-handed Fender Stratocaster left-handed by turning it upside down. This put the thick bass string on top, which suited his wild, driving, loud style.

Dick Dale and his Del-Tones are part of the foundation of the surf-music wave.

Dale experienced a reawakening when Quentin Tarantino used the driving beat of his hit "Misirlou" in the film *Pulp Fiction*. Another place you could hear Dick Dale play with fever was while riding Space Mountain at Disneyland. From 1996 to 2005, the music on this ride was Dick Dale playing an Aaron Richard composition based on *The Carnival of the Animals* by Camille Saint-Saëns. Disney has since changed this out—more's the pity.

While living in Los Angeles, I became curious about what had become of Dick Dale, and I readily found his website along with plenty of other information about what he'd been doing over the decades. From what I read, he'd built on his success by developing popular acts as his music grew. Along the way, he'd been married three times and had a son, Jimmy Dale, who is an accomplished guitar player himself. Fender sells a Jimmy Dale signature guitar alongside its signature Dick Dale model.

At the height of his fame, Dick Dale owned a huge house near the Wedge surf spot at the end of the Balboa Peninsula in Newport Beach, California, though he lost that in a tabloid-worthy divorce. By the time I went looking for him, Dale lived in a most improbable location for the King of Surf Guitar—a desolate desert wasteland north of Twentynine Palms, California. His property was located at the edge of the Marine Corps Air Ground Combat Center, the world's largest Marine Corps training base. Here, there is plenty of room to train on tanks and equipment far away from everything else.

I contacted Dick Dale through his website. Told him I'd been a fan since forever, asked when he had a performance coming up, and said I would look forward to attending. He replied like an old friend. This began an occasional correspondence about music. When my son's Boy Scout troop planned to go rock climbing on the northern side of Joshua Tree National Park, this would take us close to Dale's desert retreat.

My next message asked if I could drop by with a couple of the Scouts while we were in the vicinity. Dale responded favorably. Due to his living in the middle of nowhere, he doesn't get a lot of visitors, not out in this dusty desert moonscape, so we worked out a time. I got elaborate directions involving long, unpaved roads lacking signs or neighbors or landmarks, with instructions to keep an eye out for his airplane hangar and private runway. Being Boy Scouts, we were not afraid.

The Scout troop drove into the high desert, where we set up our tents. Saturday, we met our guides at the north entrance to Joshua Tree National Park. Joshua trees are stunning structures with thick trunks and shaggy spiked leaves.

We climbed rocks all morning, broke for lunch, then climbed some more in the afternoon. After a call to Dale, we finalized our visit. The next morning we broke camp and began our search for Dale. My son, Bennett, and one other Scout came along. Both were sixth-graders at the time. Of course they'd never heard of surf guitar or knew who we were going to meet.

We drove to Twentynine Palms, a sunburnt town with its Marine Corps vibe. From there, I followed Dale's directions, heading north toward the scrubby horizon. The farther we went, the more lunar rover I felt. Perhaps we would happen across the bones of a long-lost band of conquistadors who perished looking for a city of gold. A mile this way on a long, straight road, more miles north again toward the Marine base, into an area labeled Wonderland on the map. We had to be getting so close to the military reserve that a heavily armored vehicle might appear cresting a hill to warn us we'd wandered onto a firing range.

At long last, a sun-faded midcentury house appeared in the distance, where the view across the desert stretched all the way to the purple horizon. The sweet little runway looked long enough to land most reasonably sized private aircraft. Maybe even a fighter jet under duress, understanding they might run off the end into the desert. The largest structure on the property was an intriguing hangar.

How many rock-and-roll stars can you email to begin with? How often can you invite yourself over to their house, in the middle of freaking nowhere, to wrap up a Boy Scout campout? Which *Twilight Zone* episode could I be driving into?

The front of the house looked like any other of the era with a small front door—no grand entrance.

I rang the bell.

The man appeared. Dale had a ponytail, dyed black, and wore running shoes, teal shorts, with a solid black tank top exposing his arms to the weather.

"Hello, thanks for coming," Dale said. "How about I show you around? Give you a tour of my place."

"That'd be great." I said, and I went on to thank him profusely for the opportunity to visit.

The boys were fascinated from the start. I explained surf guitar, the whole Beach Boys invention of California, plus songs from "Wipe Out"—a song by the Surfaris with an iconic drum solo—to "Pipeline" by the Chantays in the early 1960s. The details went over their heads but they were entertained.

Mentioning the 1960s decades later to sixth-graders seemed like talking to them about Napoleon and dinosaurs. Dale loaded us into his SUV, me riding shotgun, the boys in back, and drove us around the parched earth of his desert estate. We started with a little parade down his private runway, traveling all the way to the eastern end, then turning around to drive back down the center line to the other end.

"You know this is an emergency landing strip," Dale said.

"Have you had any surprise visitors? Anybody land here just to do it?" I asked.

"No, not usually," Dale said. "My son Jimmy rode his motorcycle down the runway, used to, before he crashed his bike," Dale explained with regret in his voice. He went on about his son, an accomplished guitar player who performed with his father on occasion.

Dale drove slowly, as if to emphasize the size and uniqueness of owning this piece of the property. The original owners of the place built everything, and Dale said he was happy to find the property because he was a pilot.

"When I learned to fly, I used to cruise over the LA Basin. Looked at all the houses, all the people. It just goes on forever," he explained as we headed for the hangar near his house. "I used to own a big house at the beach."

Dale opened the enormous hangar door. "I was flying over LA one day, and looking out over it, I could see the thick layer of air pollution. Brown air. Everybody down there breathing it. I decided to move out here, away from all that."

We wandered into Dick Dale's airplane hangar as if we were adventurers in a Jules Verne story, descending into a cavern to begin a journey to the center of the earth. The inside of the sonorous barn was packed with memorabilia and plenty of toys. Huge banners, posters, even billboard signs were propped up everywhere. Posters hung from the walls, many of them from concerts in different eras.

The oldest advertising banner for Dick Dale and his Del-Tones looked twelve feet tall and was black and white. Many other signs were color, some with crashing waves and "King of the Surf Wave" or some version of that phrase. The posters highlighted different phases of Dick Dale's career. Another Del-Tones billboard dated back to the early days. Several large posters referenced his career performing with his first wife, Jeannie, in the 1970s, leading up to their blistering divorce in 1984. She was a Tahitian dancer and singer in Hawaii. They made a fortune touring the Vegas-Tahoe club circuit. Their purchases included that huge three-story, seventeen- room house in Newport Beach at the mouth of Newport Harbor.

We could have spent several hours digging through all the treasures of Dick Dale's memorabilia. After a thirty-minute tour, we took some pictures, and he showed us his Rolls Royce, a great long beast of a car with a thick coat of grit.

"I haven't started it in a while," Dale said before showing us his two airplanes. One of them a popular general aviation aircraft—a Cessna maybe. The other was an oddball plane with a pusher propeller in back that looked like an experimental aircraft. Dale made mention of flying it.

"I wrote 'Spatial Distortion'," he recalled as we stood beside one of the aircraft. "The song's about flying when you can't tell up from down. It came from my experience as a pilot."

Other knickknacks in the hangar included amps and gear he'd used in his shows. Wardrobe boxes, a couple other cars, and gadgets.

After taking a photo with my son and me, Dale asked, "Want a guitar lesson?"

Did we want a guitar lesson from the greatest guitar player in the world?

Holy smokes. Damn the torpedoes, full speed ahead.

We returned to his house, entering what would have been an ordinary midcentury suburban dwelling if nobody in particular lived there. We first saw the living room, where a window provided an unobstructed panorama of the landscape with an empty swimming pool in the foreground.

"Here, let's talk about guitar for a bit," Dale said.

He led us to an open dining room connected to the kitchen. There, a huge TV played CNN with the sound off. We situated ourselves in a small circle of chairs near the dining table.

"I only own one guitar," Dale said. Just like that, his acclaimed Fender Stratocaster appeared. He plugged it into an amplifier, and when he strummed, the coolest, smoothest, crispest, most vibrant notes I'd ever heard from an electric instrument filled the kitchen.

As he played, I began to understand how differently a musical genius like Dick Dale perceived the world. He'd mastered the physical aspects of playing. The mathematics involved. Tone, volume, impact of the pick on the strings, dynamics, the emotion he could impart. Dick Dale simply operated in a different reality than an ordinary guitar player. I've seldom encountered a person like this.

"I have a built-in tuner." Dale explained different features on the Stratocaster. At first, I thought he meant inside his head. But no, the tuner fitted into the middle of his guitar showed whether a string was sharp or flat by displaying a line of light. The strings were heavy-duty because in later years, Dale moved into a leaner, louder style, which he credited his second wife, Jill, with helping him move toward.

"I pick down on each note." He demonstrated a fast series of notes played sharp and crisp and clean, one right after the other. Every one of them down, down, down. "I work with some musicians who want to play pick up, down, up, down, but it's not crisp. Doesn't snap. It's easy to go up and down, but that's not the sound I'm looking for—not what I want."

He demonstrated this by running up and down the scale at breakneck speed, each note distinct. Sitting so close, knee to knee, we were able to hear both the sound from the string itself and the amplified note.

The boys responded with awe, asking question after question. My son had a genuine smile of wonder.

When we played a recording of one of Dale's songs later, Bennett said, "It sounds a lot better in person."

We stayed a while longer, then needed to get back home.

"Thank you for coming by. Great to meet you," Dale said and walked us out to the car.

After that, I occasionally exchanged emails with Dick Dale. When he talked about his struggle with colon cancer, he said, "At least I'm still looking down at the grass instead of up at the roots."

When he passed away on March 16, 2019, he had still not been officially inducted into the Rock & Roll Hall of Fame.

In his superb book, *The Birth of Loud,* author Ian S. Port talks about how Dick Dale worked with electric guitar entrepreneur Leo Fender to produce a bigger, richer, thumping sound from his electric guitar. Dale met with Fender continuously to improve the equipment and his performance. Dale wanted a loud, sharp guitar sound.

Port writes: "Dale jackhammered electric notes out into the ballroom, as if trying to stab the sound of his guitar through the chests of fans. His picks disintegrated on his thick guitar strings, and flurries of white plastic rained down on the checkered stage at his feet."

Chapter 18
Buying a Bow

Lessons with Mary Ann continued every Thursday at one o'clock. I practiced during the week, not quite every day, but more often than with any other instrument I've played.

The more I played, the more familiar I became with holding the cello, and the easier producing good tone became. I felt virtuous about my progress, especially how I'd become accustomed to the way the instrument shifts when I play. Positioning my fingers on the fingerboard gradually helped me land notes and understand how managing the choreography of the bow gave me confidence.

I gradually became less worried about dropping the instrument or accidently banging it up. Playing became more like spending time with an old friend rather than being trapped in a bad conversation I wanted to escape.

I also began to sense how the cello informs you how it wants to be held and moved around when played. When positioned at too steep a slant or held at an overly upright slant, the instrument rebels and becomes hard to work with. By rolling the body of the cello one way or another, the strings on the far side are either more accessible or harder to reach.

Your right arm is moving the bow in at least three dimensions, up, down, and perpendicular to the strings, while it seems like more. You are adjusting the instrument, while at the same time moving yourself into the right position to play the succession of different notes on different strings.

This, in turn, dictates how your left arm folds so your hand can hold the fingerboard in the correct orientation.

As we moved through winter, Lake Music became less hospitable. Since this end of the building was not heated or air-conditioned, the temperature felt wrong most of the time. More cans were positioned around to catch drips from the leaky roof during the rainy season.

The adjoining restaurant was dry with heat and cooling, so I suggested we move our lesson next door, which I was sure my *tico* friends would welcome. There was room in a back corner, plus we're regular Costa Rican food diners. Instead, we stayed, as Mary Ann had that inexpensive heater on the floor of her studio. We continued to leave the door open—otherwise no air would move around inside the room. However, this opens the lesson room to the hall and store area, so you learn to ignore noises, other students, or children running around, but it lets the heat out.

Once I bought my nice cello, a new wave of enthusiasm propelled my playing. My desire to hear my cello's enriched, robust sound increased the enjoyment of working through the exercise books. I found "God Save the Queen" for cello free on the internet, printed it out, and taped the two pages together, making it easy to spread out on the music stand.

Mary Ann gave me a lot of flexibility. "You're an adult, so you can do what you want," she said, though she usually told me what to do anyway. I warmed up with the C scale, then played "God Save the 'King'" for her a couple times to get a lesson going.

"Better. Try it again and make it more musical," she said.

I knew what she meant without her having to explain. After the first few weeks with my own cello, Mary Ann again had me focusing on tone and added making the playing more musically and combining that with producing a rich, appealing resonance.

My work on "Here Comes the Sun" continued. The first page of the sheet music was simple. However, the second page got into the section without lyrics, when what sounded like a whole orchestra on the recording built to a crescendo leading to the refrain. This took me a long time to work through as a beginning solo player.

"It's essential to work on tone from the start. If you're used to producing good tone from the get-go, the sound is better, and you grow in confidence," Mary Ann explained.

As I concentrated on searching for a big, rich, full, concert hall sound, Mary Ann started to drop in polite, pointed comments about my bow. Specifically, the quality of the bow that came with my cello. I knew it was at the low end of the spectrum. When I selected my cello, David Kerr had asked me about selecting a bow, but I was too overwhelmed at the time. Not knowing where to begin with bows, I waited until my current bow blocked my progress so I better understood what all a bow meant to playing well.

Mary Ann said, "There are a lot of nuances to listen for with bows. A good bow, or even a great one that works with your playing style, brings out the best in your cello. It is really easy to play with a good bow."

This brought on a flashback. The topic of having a good instrument came up many times while I worked my way through my *Rubank Elementary Method* lesson book we were using at this time. I'd used the *Rubank* book for trombone when I was a kid. The covers were the identical blue design as my current *Rubank* cello lesson book.

Mary Ann had started me out with a more advanced book, one designed for an adult beginner. I struggled with using that one for about three weeks before I bought the straightforward, step-by-step blue book from the Rubank Educational Library. All this reminded me how much I felt held back by not having the right instrument way back when.

It turned out bows are treated as instruments unto themselves, at least by cello players. They are at least half of a cello since you can't play without one.

I asked Mary Ann what I needed to know about cello bows. She dropped more pointed clues about my current bow not being all that great for a while, though this didn't get my attention. How maybe, just maybe, the bow wasn't a bow at all. The bow was a stick.

"A stick?" I asked.

"Yes, a stick," Mary Ann said in her usual easy, light tone.

"What makes it a stick?"

"Some people call a bow a stick. Sometimes saying it's a stick means it's dead, but usually they just mean it's a bow. Let's think about the qualities in a good bow," she said. "Responsiveness, flex, bounce—especially bounce." She went on to explain that not all bows have these qualities. They vary in quality. Some have no life to them, and they won't help you get the best out of your performance.

Turns out, the room to test different bows was the same room I had tried out all those cellos in a few months back. Mary Ann met me back at home base, David Kerr Violin Shop, arriving for our late-morning appointment to test out some new bows.

Steve, a tall, attentive fellow in a white dress shirt, greeted us at the front desk. Steve Banchero possessed encyclopedic knowledge about stringed instruments and opinions about what was good and bad and best about all aspects. His knowledge was helpful stuff for a beginner. "Bows! What price range did you want to try?"

A good question.

I responded, "No clue. My head is a great empty space, devoid of any knowledge of cello bows."

That cleared things up immediately.

"You're new to cello," Steve said, stating the obvious. Turned out he graduated from the Chicago School of Violin Making, in addition to his having years of experience with instruments.

"Just started playing," I said. "Obviously I'm looking for the cheapest and best. Where do we start?"

"Most affordable, not cheapest," Steve said.

"Of course, that's what I meant." I assured him I wanted to move to a good bow.

David Kerr joined Steve as they showed us back into the cello room, a familiar space from our previous visit. The room hadn't changed. Thick, quieting rugs hung on the walls. Cellos stood along all four walls, surrounding me. These were the cellos I had not selected the last time I had been here. I sensed they remembered me for passing them over. Cellos have memories, I think, and each has its own karma. I could feel this as I unpacked my own cello, which I brought to test different bows. Experiencing a bow by playing on your own instrument is important, Mary Ann told me.

Kerr slid a drawer-shaped, flat box from a special rack designed to hold them. The box was leather bound, hinged with silver latches, as if it might contain nuclear launch codes or ancient amulets. He opened the lid to reveal a dozen elegant cello bows. All appeared similar in some ways, different in others. There's no such thing as a handmade cello bow that's identical to another. The colors were brown, ranging from the blackish hue of a smoked cigar to a wispy latte umber.

The best were made of wood from the rare Brazilwood tree, which can no longer be harvested to make new bows. You can buy one of these used, but for a fancy price. I could not tell by casually looking at them which were graphite bows or those made of these endangered trees. The luthiers do a great job of making them all look the same, and I just didn't have enough experience with them.

As we went through this process, I remembered when I began seeking advice about bows, mentions of Brazilwood and Pernambuco were thrown around interchangeably. After a while, this didn't smell right. There was no consistency in the use of these terms when used by some. Those with the most knowledge praised Pernambuco and sniffed at Brazilwood for being less desirable. When I priced bows, I found the thrifty cellists saved money by buying cheaper bows made of Brazilwood. Pernambuco wood bows usually cost more. What was going on here?

After some exploration, I found several sources that agreed that the two names are different parts of the wood from the same tree. Brazilwood is the name of the tree that both Brazilwood and Pernambuco wood come from. However, Pernambuco is the heartwood of the tree and is considered stronger with more spring to it.

Brazilwood is the tree's sapwood. This is the outer ring of wood that surrounds the heartwood. Luthiers still make bows out of Brazilwood that was exported before the ban. These bows are considered clunkier feeling by some cellists, lacking the springiness to them as highly desired Pernambuco bows.

The construction of a cello bow appears deceptively simple. The main structure is the shaft, which runs from the frog to the tip. This is the "stick" part of the bow.

Kerr laid out the bows on a side table where Mary Ann was sitting. He looked them over, then left the room and returned with four more in the higher price range, stretching upward of $1,000 each. The least expensive of this selection of quality bows running $120. Looking at them all lined up on the tabletop, I couldn't tell one from another.

"Let's take them one at a time." Mary Ann sat across from me as before.

"Would you like to start with a wood bow or a composite bow?" Mary Ann looked over the bows as if considering a quiver of arrows.

"What do you suggest?" I asked, sitting with my cello, all ready to go.

"Here's a composite bow. You've been using a composite, so let's see how you think this one compares."

Although cello bows are, in theory, a standard length, they vary to a small degree in weight and balance, stiffness and flexibility, how they interact with a particular instrument, and how each one feels when you hold it in your hand. One bow seems to make playing smooth and easy, while another draws out squeaks or scratchiness, or does nothing to enhance the experience. This mystical quality present in a good bow is feel. A particular bow either feels right or it doesn't.

Mary Ann said, "You know you've found it when the bow becomes one with you and your cello. They all work together, making the instrument easy to play."

With all the different trees in the world, the idea that there is only one suited to make the great bows for violins, violas, cellos, or other string instruments seems impossible. As mentioned, the wood considered best for bows is Pernambuco. This wood can be shaped into an ideal bow with flexibility, strength, beauty, and durability by the bowmaker.

Pernambuco grows in the Brazilian rainforest and is the national tree of Brazil. Other types of wood have been tried in bow making, including ironwood, snakewood, ipe wood, and many others. But nothing has been found better than Pernambuco, which was originally used to produce a red dye.

The export or import of Pernambuco is restricted due to overharvesting—the tree is endangered. These restrictions cause dizzying complications. A musician traveling from the United States to another country is not allowed to transport a bow made of Pernambuco, or they risk its confiscation. Plantations of trees are being established on private estates, which, in theory, could be used to make bows, according to one Brazilian bow manufacturer. However, verifying the source of the wood can be difficult.

There are also sizable storehouses of Pernambuco wood, sources say, which new bows could come from. I've since talked with bow makers who purchased enough of this wood, when they could still get it, to make bows for the rest of their lives. Even so, with concern about the availability of the preferred material, new bows are being made from composites.

Composites are reinforced plastics that can be formulated to mimic the characteristics of a wooden bow. Fiberglass, graphite, and carbon fibers can be imbedded in plastic resin, giving the substrate additional strength. Fiberglass is the most common composite. Boats, car bumpers, and sometimes entire vehicles are made of fiberglass. Graphite and carbon are more expensive, lighter, can be stronger, and provide other characteristics in an attempt to duplicate a wooden bow.

Carbon fiber is also used to make cellos, which are said to be made more comfortable to play by rounding the edges and smoothing the shape. Because a carbon fiber composite doesn't react to environmental changes the way wood does, the material is resistant to damage, temperature, and humidity fluctuations. Their exterior can be easily cleaned. Plus, the same bridge can be used all year long to support the strings, instead of being changed out during the summer, which serious amateurs and professionals sometimes do to accommodate weather fluctuations.

Traditionalists say carbon fiber instruments lack the variability of wood and the rich, woody tone, which gives wooden cellos their individuality. Meanwhile, enthusiasts love them and believe they represent the future. When I asked cello luthier Michael Doran what he thought about making cellos with composites, he said, "That's going in the wrong direction." The heart of what makes violin and cello family instruments amazing is the wonderful variability of wood.

With what knowledge I'd gained to this point, I still could not, at a glance, distinguish a composite bow from one made of traditional wood. The resins used to create these bows are tinted to match the color of the wood and are patterned to suggest a wood grain.

Mary Ann picked a bow from those on the table. "Test this out. Try a scale. Listen to how it sounds. More importantly, how it feels." Mary Ann shifted forward in her chair, altogether curious about what unexpected sound I might produce.

I positioned the bow on the C string and pulled. My cello vibrated nicely and solidly, though this bow wasn't altogether better than the one I'd been using, and it didn't have much of the bounce or responsiveness Mary Ann told me to look for. I tried working my way up the scale to see if I heard a bigger, rounder tone, but the sound didn't grow.

The second bow seemed longer, even though I was assured they were all the same. This one felt more cooperative, more willing to coax the instrument along. Both bows so far had composite shafts.

A wooden bow came next. The price ascends steeply when it's made of endangered wood. I did ask the cost of some bows as we went along, starting with this one. Within the set of bows I auditioned that morning, a couple hit just short of $1,000 each. Most were in the $200 to $500 range. My concept of a bow being little more than an accessory to the cello quickly squirmed away. Bows were major big deals. I'd underestimated their importance.

When I tried a bow with a wooden shaft, Mary Ann said, "Don't look at the price. Just play it. See if it is a good combination with your cello."

This was easy enough to do. My thumb covered the price sticker when I grasped the frog and played a scale.

The frog, as the casual observer can see, is a poor excuse for a handle on the end of the cello bow. The frog's design evolved over thousands of years, though without making it easier to use, it seems. They probably began with a stick a musician found and tied a string across. Or maybe a musician tried using an archery bow on an instrument and found it improved the playing experience. We will never know.

There isn't much of a record of the earliest string instruments they are fragile and don't last. The Lyres of Ur are the oldest string instruments yet found. They date back to 2600 BC, having been placed within the tomb of Queen Puabi in the ancient city of Ur, in what is now Iraq. One of the lyres was found with the skeleton of a woman, her hands positioned as if plucking the strings.

Over time, the number of strings on these instruments increased as musicians experimented with their designs. The bow continued to evolve as ancient luthiers experimented and new ideas were introduced.

The current bow design suggests that comfort while holding the frog is not the primary design focus. The player's thumb gets wedged into the U-shaped notch and needs to stay bent with the knuckle out— not straight. Some of these notches on the bows I tested were smoother than others. With the thumb engaged, your other four fingers spread across the frog, drop over the top, and down the other side to balance the whole length of the bow from one end. The index finger is positioned to apply pressure on the bow to generate a rich tone. Some cellists play with their pinkies raised in the air as though they were sipping from a cup of tea.

Describing how this is supposed to work is more complicated than simply grasping the bow and playing. A great deal of my practice time has been spent trying to follow Mary Ann's directions about correcting my hold on the bow, while adding what I've learned by watching videos and live performances of other cello players.

From the frog, the shaft is wrapped in leather for a little over an inch. Beyond that is silver wire, tightly wound for another inch or so and soldered in place. These materials have been available since ancient times, when bow design adapted and improved. My starter bow was an economy model, wrapped with an inch of rubber instead of leather along the first section of the bow, with no silver wire or any substitute material in its place.

To complicate the mechanics of the frog, there's a tightening screw for adjusting the tension of the horsehair. It seems straightforward enough—you turn a screw to tighten the horsehair or release it. But how much tension is needed? I felt I could play for years without ever finding out.

"Tourte makes good bows," Mary Ann said as I tried one bow after another—rows of bows accumulating on my lap. "Think some of these are expensive? Well, a Tourte bow can cost more than a cello."

François Tourte is credited for developing the modern bow the same way Stradivari is known for standardizing the cello. From the age of eight, Tourte worked as a watchmaker, then shifted to apprenticing with his father's luthier shop.

From 1785 to 1790, Tourte collaborated with G.B. Viotti, a well-known violinist, to improve bow design and manufacturing. His was the golden age of innovation in bow making. Tourte is said to have destroyed any bows that weren't absolutely perfect rather than sell them.

Tourte wandered the Paris docks in search of the perfect bow wood. Portuguese colonists in Brazil exported Pernambuco to make dyes. He tried this Brazil-grown wood, and it changed bow making. One characteristic of this wood is its ability to be heated and shaped— then hold that shape. This meant a bend could be applied to a bow to add bounce and create springiness.

The tightening screw was an innovation by François Tourte, as was the hair spreader. This invention flattened the horsehair into a ribbon. Keeping the horsehair flat provides a broader surface for the hair to move over the strings and prevents tangling.

These many improvements help make a bow feel like an extension of the cellist's hand and arm. Tourte finished his bows with powdered pumice and oil rather than varnishing them. His designs are carefully copied by luthiers and have set the standard for all bows since.

Mary Ann handed me another bow, and another, and another, until we'd tried them all. I rested the bows in my lap until I'd accumulated a dozen or more. Next, we winnowed down the options by simply comparing two bows at a time. I picked one or the other during these comparisons until we were down to six contenders.

Next, I closed my eyes, and Mary Ann handed me a bow to test. This provided an opportunity to listen and focus on the feel without seeing wood or composite, new or old, and remaining unaware of the sticker price.

I didn't have a specific amount I was willing to pay, though I couldn't skip a mortgage payment to indulge my cello impulse. With reality sounding a sad minor chord, I gave the prices a glance and was surprised that four of this last group were on the low end of the price spectrum. This was good news. I'd been told that expensive bows, or pricy cellos for that matter, weren't necessarily better than more modestly priced models.

It was a composite bow. Out of all those I tried, a wood bow didn't come out on top. At least, within my price range.

Now I was playing a Chinese-made cello using a reinforced plastic bow. They were selected by me with the help of a wise, experienced teacher. When I began the process with little knowledge about cello playing, I could not have predicted this.

What could possibly get in my way now, except my own ability to put time and focus into learning to play?

Chapter 19
Musicians I Grew Up With

We had a huge high school class, the largest graduating class ever in California at the time, around 1,250 students in the graduation ceremony. A few professional musicians came out of the Will C. Crawford High School in San Diego, class of 1969. Though the talented didn't always go to the music department to learn the craft. Just as well, as I've explained.

Farley at Frontierland

A friend of mine from Crawford was a natural at playing the violin. He mastered the instrument easily, combining playing it with his easygoing personality. Gary Francisco performed with different bands until he became well known in the Southern California music community.

The first time he performed at Disneyland, he was in his twenties with his band Montezuma's Revenge. This introduced him to the organization, and in time, Disneyland hired Francisco to play the fiddle at Frontierland. There, he created the character named Farley the Fiddler. He appeared on the Golden Horseshoe stage and on the boardwalk there, where he wisecracked and played his violin. He was a fixture at Disneyland for thirty years playing his Farley character. The number of hours he spent playing the violin is incalculable, but it started with taking to the violin and sticking with it.

The Fool on the Hill

Another musician I went to high school with wasn't in the band, orchestra, or choir. He never took a music class that I was aware of. This thin, dark-haired, and unassuming teenager had a musical tilt and used to bring his guitar to school, playing during lunch. The lunch quad was an open area littered with benches. There were steps on the east side leading up to the gym. He would sit at the top of these steps, looking over the hundreds of us with sack lunches, and play his guitar. Hurtin' songs, romance-gone-wrong, the-girl-who-got-away tunes about being bruised by love were his specialty.

Because he sat up there above us, a friend of mine called him "the fool on the hill," after the lyric from a Beatles song. He had the unrequited love, sad, lyrical style pretty well figured out by the time we graduated.

Stephen Bishop moved up to Hollywood and wrote hit songs, "On and On" and "Save It For a Rainy Day" being two of them you've heard in an elevator. He wrote lyrics for Burt Bacharach and sang the title song "It Might Be You" on the movie *Tootsie*. Bish, as he likes to be known, received an Academy Award nomination for his song "Separate Lives" from the film *White Nights*. Lionel Richie won that year for the title song to the same movie.

Bish made cameos in a few movies. In *Animal House*, he's sitting on the stairs playing "Kumbaya," triggering John Belushi to grab his guitar and smash it into splinters. Yes, I went to high school with that guy. Steve, as I always called him, also appeared in cameos on TV shows, including *Laverne and Shirley,* and in other movies.

He grappled with the challenges of early success, arriving at our ten-year high school reunion delirious from his early success in show biz. Why not? He had hit tunes. He showed up wearing a white suit with white tennis shoes, glasses with round lenses, emulating John Lennon's wardrobe on the *Abbey Road* album cover. Bishop played a couple of his songs with the band the reunion committee hired. Being twenty-eight years old with hit songs under his belt, he had a lot of classmates have their pictures taken with him. He even looked at me briefly and said, "George Sorensen—I think we had a gym class together or something."

Years later, when I'd moved to LA, I invited Bish over the hill to our house in Studio City for lunch. We were midway through our forties at this point, and his songwriting had slowed. He brought up the phase he was going through back at that reunion years ago, admitting he was still a kid and acting like one. Which was the honest truth. Bish dressed ordinarily when we met, sported an everyday haircut, but still had an LA-energy about him. He grew into a veteran songwriter with his compositions recorded by Phil Collins, Barbra Streisand, Eric Clapton, Kenny Loggins, Beyoncé, Art Garfunkel, Pavarotti, David Crosby, and many others. He's been nominated for Grammies and an Academy Award.

Trombone at the Olympics

The trombone player I sat next to all through my school band days, six long years of secondary school, was Dan Reagan. We shared a music stand all that time and talked about his big Catholic family and why they kept adding all those brothers and sisters.

Dan didn't finish college initially but ended up playing slide trombone professionally. He toured with Marc Anthony's band for a long time, in addition to other professional groups. Anthony is a top-selling salsa singer with a good-size musical ensemble, who most famously married actor, singer, and producer Jennifer Lopez, known as JLo.

Dan was at the periphery of all that show biz barking-at-the-moon. He even played trombone outdoors in the snow at the Olympics in Salt Lake City, backing Anthony's performance, saying, "It was impossible to play in town with the cold."

Last I saw Dan was in New York City, where he lived with his wife and young kids in an artist co-op and was studying for his credential to teach high school.

The Baritone Across the Street

Finding someone with an interest in music shows up where you least expect it. We bought a house on the LA River in Studio City. It was a quiet street, walking distance to Universal Studios. We found the neighbors edgy in an LA kind of way. Everyone seemed angry all the time, but weren't aware of how they acted out.

I was changing my kid's diaper one day when I heard a brass instrument playing in the street in front of my house, some type of horn. When I went outside to investigate, I saw an older neighbor standing in his driveway, playing a baritone—which is made of coiled tubing, a good-size flared bell, and plays the same music as a trombone. The man blowing the horn had been retired from running the presses at the *LA Times* for a few years. I'd met him briefly when we first moved there and was told that he lived with his second wife, next door to his ex-wife. When he divorced, he simply moved one house to the left and started over. He was the most pleasant of the folks on our short block of nutcases.

Music being a universal language, even in the angst-stricken San Fernando Valley, I fetched the old E-flat tuba I kept as a conversation starter from the living room. I'd had this brass-wind for years, purchased from the Minnesota Orchestra's lead tuba player, after searching for an affordable used one to have around for fun.

I took the tuba out to my front yard, aimed, and blasted a bunch of notes back across the street. The baritone player startled. The tuba easily overpowered the baritone due to size, even when played by an incompetent former trombone player like me, who could only fake playing a tune on a buzz-your-lips instrument.

We became fast friends when he explained, "After I retired, I started to play with a brass band. It is great fun making music with a group of hard-working amateur musicians. I'm having the time of my life."

We never would have been connected without an interest in these instruments and the willingness to take them out into the street. Musicians are everywhere.

Chapter 20
Instruments of Momentary Interest

As we know by now, the cello wasn't my first fascination with instruments. There were many excursions to music stores resulting in the production of organized sound. Here are a few examples of these diversions.

Bagpipes

In a weak musical moment, when my kids were young and I was a stay-at-home dad, I thought I might amuse them by playing the bagpipes. These are instruments of parades and funeral processions, to salute dignitaries, and perhaps for entertaining children. Bagpipes amplify whatever feeling you're having at the moment. If you're happy, the bagpipes will make you joyful. Find yourself sad, the pipes give your sadness more depth and meaning.

At a medical school commencement I attended recently, six pipers and a drummer marched before the graduates, playing them in and out of the ceremony. This enriched the sense of pageantry at the event, adding to all the caps and gowns during the hooding of the new physicians.

I thought I'd like to try inflating one of these instruments and perhaps playing "Kilt is My Delight," "High Road to Gairloch," "Farewell to Gibraltar," "Because He Was a Bonny Lad," or another favorite on the pipes while strolling in my neighborhood, creating a flurry of unpredictable responses from the curious and the annoyed. The ingenuity of the titles alone seemed enough reason to play bagpipe songs. However, there are obstacles to interacting with this octopus-inspired invention. The expense of purchasing a set of pipes didn't make a lot of sense if I was just going to explore the notion.

After some investigation, I found a store in Claremont, California, that catered to offbeat music. Folk Music Center Museum and Store sells alternative instruments from all around the world, stocking everything from African djembe drums to Peruvian flutes to lute strings. This community, situated some twenty-five miles or so east of Pasadena, is home to the five Claremont Colleges—Pitzer, Pomona, Scripps, Mudd, and Claremont McKenna. With all the college students and free-thinking individuals, a folk music store is sustainable.

A woman wearing a comfortable hand-woven sarong with bold stripes sold me a practice bagpipe chanter, as if it were no surprise someone would wander in asking for one. Most music store employees would blankly stare back at you if you asked about this sort of thing. But not in Claremont.

The chanter is the bottom part of the bagpipes, that looks like a recorder, the wooden flute kids play, used to practice. The player blows in at the top of this simple wooden tube and fingers the notes, the way they might on a clarinet. I never knew such a thing as a chanter existed, though it makes a lot of sense, considering how loud bagpipes can get. When practicing the pipes, it's good to have a way to quietly approach the whole experience.

Chanters lack the drone notes that produce the majestic wall of sound that carries across the highlands. I also bought a bagpipe fingering book and could play a couple familiar tunes after nonchalantly practicing a short bit. The main obstacle to playing is the enormous volume of air you have to push through this instrument to make it work. While the airbag in the actual bagpipes solves some of this challenge, piper players tell me this process takes getting used to.

I got lightheaded and had to sit down every time I tried.

Didgeridoo

On a visit to Sydney, I heard the band Galapagos Duck play several times. During one of their numbers, the trombone player brought out a didgeridoo and played it with jazz styling. This performance was effective and drew great applause. Fueled by this inspiration, I bought a didgeridoo from a store at The Rocks, a shopping area at one end of the Sydney Harbor Bridge. I had the choice between didgeridoos painted with traditional materials—which were dusty and, in time, would wear off—or acrylic paint. I picked the acrylic since I intended to play it, which would cause the traditional coloring to fade with so much handling.

A didgeridoo is fashioned from a hollowed-out tree branch and coated with wax around the end where you buzz your lips to produce the sound—not unlike the tuba or trombone in that regard. The instrument is thought to have originated in Australia about one thousand years ago, as there are rock paintings dating to that time depicting people playing it. In the wild, termites hollow out the eucalyptus branch, sometimes creating a flared end as they eat their way through the center. A didgeridoo with a flared end tends to play a larger range of notes than a straight one. The organic buzzing sounds have an earthy resonance—sounding spooky, soothing, mysterious, bee-like, an unearthly rumbling.

I kept mine in the living room with the tuba I didn't know how to play, until we met an Australian couple while living in LA. When their ten-year-old son saw the instrument and asked, "What's that?" his mother grew alarmed that he had never heard of what must be the Land Down Under's national instrument. I gave it to him. Though playing the didgeridoo occasionally was fun, I was surprised how many people who walked into our living room and saw it felt they ought to pick it up and play it—grabbing the thing and buzzing into it without asking.

I suppose the uninitiated were comfortable doing this because, it seems on some level to them at least, little more than a painted stick with a hole in both ends.

Concertina

On my first trip to Europe, back in 1968, my fascination with odd instruments had already been well established, and I'd become interested in the concertina. I'm not sure where this came from, as I don't remember seeing one of these squeeze boxes in person. They are part of the accordion family, but quite small, with a barrel shape and squared-off sides. Concertinas show up in old pirate movies, when a crusty old salt pulls one out of his sea chest and plays to pass the time—perhaps accompanying sea shanties, which have renewed in popularity these days. Some colleges have clubs devoted to singing sailing songs.

I have always enjoyed the spirit of these shanties. The first one leaving an impression was in the Disney classic *20,000 Leagues Under the Sea*. In it, Kirk Douglas plays Ned Land, a harpooner, who leads the crew in singing the tune "Whale of a Tale," while he plays the guitar. Following along behind him is another sailor playing a concertina. This is a great movie, and the scene is memorable.

When my kids were little, we used to watch this movie, looking forward to the scene with the song. In one line, a mermaid is described as having "a nose just like a rudder." I told my five-year-old daughter that if she learned all the words and could sing along with the movie, it would help her get into college. Kenzy is now in her thirties and can still sing every verse, which I hope she believes will be an increasingly useful skill. Of course, it would have helped her get into college if they'd asked her to sing a sea shanty during the interview. Or inquired about false promises her father made while she was growing up.

When in Amsterdam, I asked if there might be a place that sold concertinas. That led us to a music store on the second floor of a building beside a narrow canal. A sign pointed up a flight of narrow stairs, where we entered a small music shop. I asked the balding man at the desk if he sold what I was looking for. He responded, "Relax, you are in Europe now. Concertinas are not so unusual here."

He retreated to a room in back, returned with a box—round with six flat sides. He let me unpack the concertina. Both ends of the device were a decorated metal and covered with white push buttons. None of the buttons were labeled, though the instrument came with an instruction book that included a bunch of songs. To play, you fit your hands into narrow leather straps on each side. These make it easy to pull open and push closed the internal bellows box to move air through the reeds inside. It played all the same, whether you squished or expanded the concertina. The left-hand buttons played bass, and the right hand played the high notes.

We took it home with a feeling of satisfaction. At one point, I could play a couple tunes in the book. Pressing buttons on each side at the same time while pulling it apart with both hands, then pushing it together, all the time. I sounded just the way I imagined, jolly, perky, upbeat—as I'd seen it in the movies. Concertinas are fun instruments, and I kept mine for years, more as a work of art than an instrument with much depth.

The ACME Thunderer

Another instrument I once performed on played one note: a sharp whistle. I used this whistle to set the tempo for the entire band—my high school marching band—when going forward, stopping, playing music, turning corners, and performing halftime shows at football games.

ACME Thunderer is the whistle every drum major used—metal, sturdy, and sharp, as a well-designed whistle should be. They hang around the neck of the drum major by a lanyard. It is a musical instrument.

Four whistles started the band playing or marching, depending upon the circumstances. One long whistle alerted the musicians we were going to play a song or march or both march and play at the same time. Specific baton gestures used with the whistle, like pointing the baton in the direction we would march, also helped.

The whistle could easily be heard by everybody marching in a parade or on the football field during a halftime show. During our performances, the girls drill team also followed the whistle commands. Dozens and dozens of girls joined the drill team in those days. Their uniform included a short blue, red, and white dress with a fringed skirt, fancy white cowgirl boots with tassels, and cowgirl hats. We were the Crawford Colts, so this outfit captured the school mascot and spirit.

One judge inspected uniforms. "Dirty whistle" he wrote on the inspection form. I had not considered how much debris could anchor itself inside the mouthpiece and barrel of an ACME Thunderer. "Looks like an army camped in there," somebody said later.

I scrubbed the thing out with a pipe cleaner, and after that, I kept it clean as a whistle.

Chapter 21
A Cello Takes a Bullet for Bond

Bond ... James Bond got into a squabble with Soviet bad guys in *The Living Daylights*, with a cello playing a prominent supporting role. In the 1989 film starring Timothy Dalton as 007, Maryam d'Abo plays a double-crossing KGB sniper who complicates matters.

Bond is sent to deal with an assassin, only to learn d'Abo is also a cello soloist in a symphony orchestra. Naturally, he becomes entangled with her, and soon enough, they're being chased down cobblestone streets and across the Swiss mountain landscape. At one point, their adventure is delayed because she forgot her cello and they have to go back for it.

As Bond struggles to cram the instrument into the minute backseat of his Aston Martin, he quips, "Why couldn't you have picked the violin?"

They escape to a ski resort, where they're cornered with no possibility of escape. Bond uses rockets built into his Aston Martin to vault an enemy stronghold, then glides down a ski slope. They are chased downhill, only to get stuck in deep snow with no options. Bond takes the cello out of the car and uses it, still in its case, as a toboggan for the two of them to slalom to safety. The cello even takes a bullet for Bond, saving his life.

If you would like to visit this cello, along with the case used in the movie, you can. It's on display at the National Motor Museum in the village of Beaulieu, Hampshire, in England. There, you can see where skis were put on the bottom of the case and handles were attached to the side for the scene. The cello also has a bullet hole through it.

Chapter 22
The Reason for Rosin

Weekly cello lessons with Mary Ann ambled along. I improved a little each time we met, which was evident to both of us. She'd point out when I managed to make my way through pieces, declaring, "You couldn't do that before."

When I pulled out the music for "Here Comes the Sun," I could not yet generate the sound the way I heard it in my memory. The words that come to mind for what I wanted it to sound like when I played were: unusually elegant, full of energy, driving movement, delightful, and more. My ability to get the notes in the right order and keep time gave me a deep, warm glow.

I did understand my level of growth at this point. I was learning how to coordinate hands, arms, posture, and positioning the cello so the instrument moved with me, rather than trying to escape my grasp as it had in the beginning. The cello became more familiar and required less effort to control, helping me play that much better. The addition of the new bow added a layer to my lessons, as I found the fit far more cooperative than my first student bow. I dragged it across the strings with greater confidence, finding it easier to play. Not easy, just easier.

Mary Ann didn't tell me any far-reaching plans about what sort of cello player she envisioned me to be or what we'd cover next. I just kept asking questions, which would lead her to give me some new insight into playing when I was ready.

As lessons continued, I spent more time exploring professional cello performances, interviews, luthiers, and instruction videos available from a multitude of sources. Some of these online lessons were not much help. A fair number were done by earnest amateurs in an attempt to provide instruction for beginners. They were often made by a young cellist in their bedroom with a lousy microphone. They sometimes had a weird and urgent energy to them, or the player pretended to be casual when they were clearly tense to be on camera.

Most of these do-it-yourself videos covered the same six or eight biggest mistakes beginners make, repeating recommendations about keeping your feet flat on the floor and your bow straight. Basic stuff. A precious few didn't realize they left the bathroom door open in the background, as they sit with their cello admonishing everyone to pay attention. Some instructional videos set the right tone. They were done professionally with quality sound and staging.

But a new problem sprang up. I was struggling with my bow.

After playing with my new bow for a few weeks, it started skidding across the strings. I applied more pressure on the bow, which usually cures the screeching problem, as this action increases the amount of drag on the strings. But that didn't work.

"You need to rosin your bow," Mary Ann said, then explained how rosin on the bow improves drag on the strings.

Amazing I'd gone this long without adding any.

I located the bar-shaped rosin included in the cello starter kit Lake Music sold me when I began that first lesson. The kit amounted to three unexceptional items in a plastic bag: a tiny bottle of cello polish I'll never use, a polishing cloth, and a chunk of rosin. The honey-brown rosin filled a slotted piece of wood an inch-and-a-half long and the width of a cello bow. The rosin was as brittle as glass.

"Rosin." I held out what I had. "How's this?"

"It's fine for students," Mary Ann said, then described how they pour the rosin into a long piece of wood like this, let it harden, then cut it into little pieces, making it easy for young musicians to hold onto. When they drop the rosin—as they do—it cracks, but the wood holds it together.

"I already dropped mine," I reported, that being obvious. My rosin showed a bunch of cracks and looked like a fractured ice cube.

"It'll work," Mary Ann said.

"Aren't there better ones?" I asked.

This opened a floodgate to Mary Ann's knowledge of rosin.

"There are all sorts of rosin. I like French Jade. There are plenty of others. German brands are good. You can experiment and see what works for you."

Rosin is refined tree sap. Maple syrup, of course, is tree sap that is delicious on pancakes. Rubber is tree sap too, and millions of tires are made from rubber tree sap. Different tree species make sap to suit their own needs, and in turn, we humans find our own uses. Pine tree sap is sticky, and stickiness is what the horsehair on the bow needs to grab onto the strings. Pine tree sap or resin has been used to make rosin for hundreds of years. "Don't confuse resin with rosin," Mary Ann warned me.

In the early years of my writing career, I did a lot of work for the 3M company when I lived in St. Paul, Minnesota. 3M is famous for thin film technologies, including adhesives, especially their well-known brand, Scotch tape. Some tape you apply with the intention of lifting it up again and moving it somewhere else. You don't want a tight hold. At the other end of the adhesive scale is duct tape—meant to stay put.

The adhesive of each product is adjusted to deliver these qualities, which are called "tack-and-release properties." Do you want the stickiness to hold on a little or a lot?

The tack of a good rosin should grab on when it coats the bow's horsehair; there's enough drag to vibrate the strings as it releases. If it doesn't grab enough or won't let go with the right amount of drag, it isn't going to work satisfactorily.

Cello players state their preference for one rosin over another with the fervor of Manhattan drinkers arguing about the advantage of adding an orange peel over a cherry to their cocktail.

I fled to my local source of truth in all cello matters, especially to learn more about the cello bow. Jenelle Steele came down from the repair shop, when I arrived in the late afternoon at the Kerr Violin Shop. She wore a heavy-duty canvas apron, the type serious woodworkers might wear, over a long-sleeved flannel shirt. Flannel is a familiar look during an Oregon winter.

The repair shop is up a short flight of stairs, behind the front desk where the loan department might have been when the building was a bank. It must have been where customers interviewed with loan officers to process their mortgage applications but now had workbenches to deal with instrument repairs.

"Cello rosin," I said.

Jenelle replied, "We have plenty. What do you like?"

"I'm clueless," I said, though Jenelle certainly realized this immediately, as she was inordinately patient answering my questions.

"Where would you like to start?" she asked.

"I was told to check out French Jade and German rosins," I in-
formed her. "I also heard someone makes rosin in Oregon." There are
pine trees all over the place up here, so logically the ocean of sap
seemed ready to be tapped and turned into rosin.

"Oregon rosin? Hadn't heard that," Jenelle said. It turned out
there was no such thing.

She pulled open a big drawer on the back of the counter. It appeared so deep and wide it could have held a basketball with room
left over. Dividers segmented the space with each holding a different
rosin type.

"I am a cello player myself." Jenelle pulled out several rosin
brands, setting them on the counter.

Each came wrapped as if vying to be the prettiest present at a bath
boutique—they looked that fancy. These rosins could easily be mis-
taken for pricey soaps or even a small tub of caviar from an exotic part
of the world.

"Here's the French Jade your teacher raved about." Jenelle slid the
green box toward me.

This rosin was jade green of course. Inside, a round, thick shape
hid in a dark olive-colored cloth, making it seem mysterious or precious or perhaps overdressed.

"This will tint the horsehair on your bow green. I change bow hair
and see the color it leaves." Jenelle brought the rosin to her nose.
"Most of these don't have much of a smell."

She was correct. When I put my nose to them, I expected a big pine
tree scent, though it was barely there. The resin colors varied from
light yellow to a dark amber, aside from the jade green, which stood
out from the selections.

"What rosin do you use?" I asked.

"For my cello, I've used different rosins. There are some popular
American brands." Jenelle then said, as if divulging a secret, "I got a
special rosin from a friend, and I'm trying that."

"Do you carry that special brand?" I asked, as this sounded like a
mysterious type of rosin that would improve my playing.

"Oh, no. It's impossible to get. You have to get on a list. It's only
available in small quantities. Sells out fast. If you don't buy it once

you reserve it, they take you off the list," Jenelle explained, as if protecting secret nuclear codes. "High demand with a short supply."

I picked out three rosins to try, the French Jade—how could anyone resist?—plus two other brands based on the elegance of their artistic packaging.

The American-made rosin brands were packaged to be more practical looking and far less intriguing. One came in a loose-fitting cloth, like a pocket torn off a bathrobe. That rosin lacked the swanky appeal of the European brands and could never be sold in a fancy store. I hadn't anticipated that pine tree sap could be so refined or marketed in the style of fancy perfume or raised to the level of a Hermès scarf or bauble from Tiffany.

I tried all three of these rosins I purchased over several months. After trying them, I found the French Jade produced a cloud of rosin dust. The Millant Deroux rosin, also from France, didn't seem to add enough grip. My favorite became the Pirastro Gold rosin, made in Germany, as it had a better feel to it, the right stickiness, didn't give off as much dust, and came in an enchanting amber-red hue. I will try others as time goes by.

Chapter 23
Rehairing a Bow

Cellists tell sad stories about their instruments getting stepped on, holes punched into them, broken necks, tuning peg problems. Something as simple as dropping a bow on an instrument can leave a deep scratch. Most cosmetic problems you just live with, while others require major work. Then there are regular maintenance issues, including something as simple as monitoring the condition of the hair on the bow. Rehairing a bow, I was told, is something that needs to happen about once a year, which simply means that your cello bow must have its horsehair replaced.

This sounded so curious and weird I wanted to see how it was done.

I arranged to meet with Jenelle, the luthier and cello player who helped me pick out rosin. She is great to work with, quite knowledgeable, and willing to answer my endless stream of questions. When I arrived at Kerr Violins, she met me at the desk wearing the same heavy work apron as before. "I've just started rehairing a bow. Let's take a look at it." She led me up the stairs.

The stairs behind the front counter took us to the repair room that spread down the length of the building. A massive wall of windows lets in all the light a Portland spring day can muster. This is the heart of Pacific Northwest overcast country, where the sun doesn't reliably appear until the Fourth of July each year. Repairs were being conducted that day by Jenelle and two other luthiers. One wore a pair of magnifying glasses that looked like little binoculars to probe the inner workings of a violin. Another changed out some strings.

All the wooden instruments warmed up the look of the place, the same way wood paneling adds atmosphere to a swanky bar at a supper club. Dozens of violins hung in rows up high along the ceiling.

Each one of them told its own story in its scrapes and nicks. Some of these were obviously broken, while others looked like they simply needed a rest.

On the wooden worktable where Jenelle found space, a cello with its top pried off took up a lot of real estate.

I pulled over a stool to watch Jenelle work. Before her, a simple stand held a cello bow in the process of being rehaired. The old strands of hair had been removed, leaving the rest of the bow looking incomplete, like there's something wrong with it, the way a sailboat looks without a mast.

"Why does a bow need new hair?" I studied the structure of the shaft, the elegant curve that provides a structure for suspending the strands of Mongolian horsehair.

"You rehair your bow when it stops gripping the strings. Individual hairs break off as you play, but usually, about once a year, a bow needs new hair," Jenelle said as she worked. "Possibly more often if you're a professional playing all the time."

She used a razor-sharp wood chisel to create a minute wood block. The block was a little smaller than the size of the eraser at the end of a pencil. She tried fitting the block into the notch that holds the bundle of hair at the tip of the bow. The piece didn't fit, so she shaved away thin layers until it took on a keystone shape and sat in the opening to hold one end of the bundle of hair in place.

"You've heard of Tourte, the French bow designer. His designs are standard." She pointed out the silver wire wrapped around the wood by the frog to protect your hand and help balance the bow. Violin bows weigh sixty grams. Viola bows seventy grams. Cello bows eighty grams. "You always want to test the bounce of the bow. Bounce is good. It makes the bow feel alive. The bow is a huge part of the instrument."

Jenelle is another luthier who went to the Violin Making School of America where repair classes were a summer program. She started playing cello at age twelve because a friend played. Now she plays with a community chamber orchestra and repairs instruments a few days a week.

"After studying to be a luthier, I realized you must have a pretty huge amount of knowledge to be in this business. There is a richness of histories in the work, and you meet interesting people," she explained.

The bow being rehaired was worth over four thousand dollars. The value of an instrument, or in this case the bow, determines what you do to repair it. A less expensive instrument may not be worth repairing if the damage is too great. My bow cost less than the price of rehairing it, so I'll have to look at my options when the time comes.

Once the tiny wooden block fit the way she wanted, Jenelle rolled her chair over to a wire stand holding three bunches of horsehair. Each bunch had a different color of hair. One looked gray, another blond, with the third a shade in between. The bundles appeared like clean, well-ordered horsetails, which is what they were. Sourcing good horsehair is quite a business with a lot of trading among Mongolia's neighbors. There's a world market for quality horsetail, which is carefully sorted and organized for shipment. Other cold countries, including Canada, produce the type of horsehair used for bows, but Mongolia has the one everybody's after.

"Mongolian horsehair." Jenelle said as she picked through the lighter colored bunch hanging together. She examined the hair fastidiously before making an experienced estimate of how much was needed, pulled a bunch free, then made a cut with scissors. She tied a knot in one end of the bundle to secure it.

"I learned to make this knot from a Polish man whose family made sausages." She tested how the end of the bundle fit into the square notch under the tip of the bow. It fit perfectly, so she smoothed the bundle and used a peculiar little comb to eliminate snags. Once done, Jenelle added a dot of white glue to the knot before placing it in the notch. The little wooden block went over the bundle of hair. By pulling on the bundle, the block tipped into place, securing the end. A flat tip plate slid in across that end to finish one end of the operation.

What first looked like a bare shaft of wood began to reappear as a complete bow. Next, Jenelle stretched the other end of the horsehair across to the frog end of the bow—tightening the horsehair straight across the length of the bow, between the tip, to the ferrule on the frog. This is the metal piece that holds and flattens the hairs on the end the player grips. Flattening the strings provides the cellist with more predictable results and the ability to tilt the bow to achieve a more nuanced performance.

A gauge helped measure the exact length the finished bundle of hair needed to be. She cut along that line. This end got the same sausage-maker's knot and another dot of glue. The knot disappeared under the ferrule with another small block to hold it.

With a new set of hair on the completed bow, Jenelle hung it to dry.

Chapter 24
That Evening in Spain

The cello had been my companion for over six months since the first lightning bug of interest appeared on the Camino. I'd been obsessing about it becoming a preoccupation, so I thought it time to revisit my original inspiration for better perspective.

Much as the cello became a fixture in our house, Susan never much mentioned it. Occasionally when I worked my way through a lesson book while practicing, she might say, "It's nice to hear you play." Nothing more than that.

We did start going to many more concerts since I began playing. Mary Ann pointed us to one of the small community orchestras. The Tualatin Valley Symphony was a volunteer community orchestra with a group of good musicians and performed in smaller churches. Another, the Portland Columbia Symphony Orchestra, changed its name over the years and just swapped it out again, for some reason, to Orchestra Nova Northwest and refers to itself as ONN. This ensemble plays in large, high-ceiling churches.

We attended small concerts in libraries with stray musicians from the Oregon Symphony. These are free so the music will be heard in neighborhoods and accessible to everyone who wants to listen. At all these concerts, I would sit as close as I could, or at least with a good view of the cello players, to study how they played. The Oregon Symphony is the big dog in town, but I'd never been to one of their concerts, frankly. I have no reason for not going, other than the difficulty of finding a parking place in downtown Portland and being unable to get a ticket close enough to watch the cello players.

I'd check Yo-Yo Ma's website when I thought of it to see if I could snag tickets for one of his performances. Every time I tried to buy tickets for his shows, they were sold out. Months and months in advance, not a single seat anywhere near me was available, and most venues didn't even bother with waitlists, he was so popular. Nearly a year out, and they were all sold out. Even if I had found tickets, the prices approached rock-and-roll concert prices, and seemed as hard to find.

This left me enjoying the smaller orchestras and chamber ensembles so much more. The tinier the group, the more enjoyable. Susan would come along to some of these events, which seemed to help her understanding of why I found the cello so intriguing.

After a concert by one small ensemble in a public library, I told Susan I'd like to contact the Spanish cellist, the lecturer we saw on the Camino.

"You want to tell him you started playing the cello?" Susan asked.

"I think he'd be interested," I said. "I want to tell him how he sparked my interest in the instrument. Maybe he has some advice or insight he could give me. I could understand more about his devotion to the instrument, that sort of thing."

"Go ahead," Susan said.

"Do you remember his name?" I asked.

Susan journals relentlessly, adding stickers, artwork, ticket stubs, as she makes notes in little bound books. "Give me a minute." She ran off to her two desks, side tables, bookcases, file boxes, future quilting project materials, and hotchpotch that consume space in our downstairs family room.

"Carlos Ariel Gracia Baez is the cello guy." Susan came back within the blink of an eye.

When I heard "Carlos Ariel Gracia Baez," it made me want to snap my fingers and dance.

I fled to GoDaddy, entering his name, which returned several million men with nearly identical names, from Buenos Aires to Los Angeles and across the world's Spanish-speaking diaspora. Carlos Ariel Gracia Baez is a mucho popular name. The common name *John* in English must translate to *Carlos Ariel Gracia Baez* in Spanish, there were so many of them.

With some effort refining my search, the image of my Carlos appeared. A photo of the swarthy cellist leaning on a medieval bridge in a breeze popped up. His shoulder-length hair tousled with a rhapsody of artistic introspection. He looked more swashbuckling than I'd remembered. Massive black curls heaved in the Spanish wind. How could I get back in touch with this artiste to tell him what an effect his performance had on me and to hear what he had to say?

While the internet can't be trusted about much of anything, it can be helpful in locating a reputable member of the global cello community. Cello players do not hide, though they may be shy. I tried different methods to get a message to Carlos until he wrote back. In a few days, we tried one method to talk, and when that didn't work, juggled things until we managed to set up a video chat.

Carlos filled the screen as he adjusted the distance between his face and phone at his home in Santiago de Compostela. His nose predominated the screen. The dashing beard. Long black hair tied back. He'd just finished giving a cello lesson. He looked just the way I'd hoped—energizing with a ruffled animation.

"I am honored I inspired you," Carlos began. "Yes, I do remember you. No one else ever asked me to play all the Brandenburgs by myself."

"You gave the perfect response by playing the theme from each one of them," I replied. He asked about my journey playing different instruments, and I told him about all the lessons I took over the years and how I could never get a good tone in the band. I asked, "Carlos, tell me something. Why am I all of a sudden so taken by the cello?"

"Because you've always been interested in music. You sing, played trombone and piano, guitar. The cello is another means of expression for you," Carlos said. "I play cello with passion and have concentrated on musical things since I was seven."

"I can tell," I said.

"The cello is a very close friend. I try to make it sing. I play beautiful melodies with it. Bach, you know, wrote six suites. Fantastic pieces for cello. Bach suites are a miracle." He explained how the *Bach Cello Suites* were forgotten until the early 1900s. Neglected as simple studies. Pablo Casals found and performed them, brought them back to life. They are now considered a mainstay of a serious cellist's repertory.

"Pablo Casals inspired me tremendously when I was a boy," Carlos said. "Casals was one of the dominant musicians of the twentieth century."

Pablo Casals was considered the greatest cellist who ever lived, at the time of his death. He grew up in Tarragona, Spain, the son of a church organist and choir director. He started playing the cello at eleven years old and studied in Barcelona for many years.

When Francisco Franco forced his way to power in Spain, Casals moved across the border to France, promising not to return until democracy was restored. He also refused to perform in countries that recognized the Spanish government, including the United States.

Casals toured extensively from a young age. He performed for Queen Victoria in London in 1899. Played for President Teddy Roosevelt in 1904, along with additional White House performances, including for President Kennedy in 1961. He eventually settled in Puerto Rico. There, he energized the musical environment by founding the Conservatory of Music of Puerto Rico and the Puerto Rico Symphony Orchestra.

Among Casals' most notable quotes is, "The art of interpretation is not to play what is written." Also, upon being asked why, at the age of ninety-three, he still devoted three hours a day to practicing, he said, "I'm beginning to notice some improvement."

He became known as an ambassador for peace, was awarded the Presidential Medal of Freedom, and traveled to Washington, D.C., to receive it.

Casals married his third wife, Marta Montañez Martinez, a twenty-year-old, at the age of eighty. When concerns were raised about their age difference, Casals replied, "I look at it this way—if she dies, she dies."

I watched Carlos wander from room to room through his apartment during our call, moving from light to dark to light to shadows. This is what a Spanish cellist should look like—artistic and wrestling with dark and light, I supposed.

Carlos is a citizen of both Mexico and Spain. He studied at the London School of Music and served as a postgraduate conductor at the Royal Scottish Academy of Music and Drama. He also conducted the Athens State Orchestra during London Symphony master class sessions and with other institutions, including the University of Santiago de Compostela.

Carlos spoke about the many aspects of playing the cello as he went on about the extended community of cellists. As with every person associated with the cello I spoke to, he felt connected somehow to every other cellist in the world. Carlos talked about his sense that the cello occupies a universal place in the soul. About this resonating wooden box with the capacity to calm and mesmerize, taking people on both a musical and spiritual journey.

"Taking the right posture is essential." Carlos walked around his home as he talked. "Sit in such a way so the center of balance is right in the middle. Height of the chair is important. Your thighs should be parallel to the floor. Be comfortable."

He reiterated, "Keep the cello between your knees at an angle where the pegs don't get in the way of your head. Your shoulders should not be too high.

"Your right hand is most important," Carlos said. "I teach the left and the right hands separately, then how to coordinate them. It can be difficult to bring them together. The right hand is most important. It's the sound articulation, the singing part of the music. The bow creates the voice."

Carlos' additional advice included making sure the cellist has no stiff joints. Don't over-clamp your thumbs. Make sure to play relaxed. When you practice, simply concentrate on specific issues, focusing on basic tasks.

"Adults think too much about everything. They over-reason everything. This helps prevent that."

Carlos emphasized the importance of concentration while practicing, then told a story from a friend in the BBC Orchestra. The recommendation from this friend was that, while it's important to practice, know when to stop. Play with all your senses; otherwise practicing is a waste of time. Once developed, bad habits take a long time to break. Set small goals every day, the first being the right posture. Find what's normal and natural for you.

Chapter 25
Stan the Panda Man

The more I've played the cello, the more I'm reminded of the big stuffed animals at the county fair, the unusually large plush bears especially. The ones as big as you when you're a kid. My favorites were the stuffed pandas.

We called them "panda bears" back then, and the giant panda, it turns out, is a true bear, part of the family Ursidae. For a while, the rumor was it was some kind of raccoon or from the rodent family, but that's not true. They are bears.

I wanted a stuffed panda when I first saw them when a little kid at the San Diego County Fair. This annual gathering at the Del Mar Racetrack ran for a week or so, ending the Fourth of July. The grounds around the horse track and stables included exhibit halls with an expanse of concrete for carnival rides and parking. The fair was an important highlight of the summer. One year I even saw Jimmy Durante perform on stage there. He lived in Del Mar, near the track.

In the midway area were the spinning rides and a house of mirrors, the types that move from one fair to another throughout the year, encumbered with the feeling they were operated by recently released convicts. I remember eating a barbeque sandwich drenched in a sauce there when I was all of eight. The ocean of this sauce seemed meant to disguise the mystery meat bought by a low-cost culinary operation. Soon after eating the thing, I spent an hour heaving my guts out in the bushes next to the merry-go-round, all the lights flashing and music pounding. What a magical childhood memory.

We had driven to the fair in my godfather's brand-new Ford Thunderbird—the model with fins and taillights resembling rockets. He was painfully on edge during the ride home, deathly afraid I'd bazooka the back of his seat, if my stomach had anything left to give. For the record, I didn't.

The terror of that ride aside, I longed for the great big panda I'd seen in the lineup at one of the arcade games. He was nearly as tall as I was, or seemed so, black and white, with eyes that seemed to follow me as I walked by. Here, you threw a baseball at a stack of weighted metal milk bottles. Three throws for twenty-five cents. Knock enough bottles down, you get a panda.

Little kids seldom got anywhere with this game. If they had the power, they didn't have good aim. As with all these games, the guys running them don't expect anybody to win and are unhappy if you do.

My dad curated the show at the Fine Arts Building at the fair. This being the height of midcentury design, there were a lot of horizontal surfaces, plywood sheets low to the floor, pottery, drawings, paintings, and artwork in a juried show. One year a wood carver chiseled a matador out of a tall tree trunk. When finished, the carving became a fixture at a local high school that had a matador mascot.

After I got interested in these pandas, a friend of my dad appeared. Stan was part of the art community, a student learning to be an art teacher. He rode in our car with us to the fair that year. When we were stuck at a long red light, he jumped out, ran over, and pushed the crosswalk button to speed things up, then ran back to the car. He acted like a kid, which endeared me to him.

"You know," I heard Stan brag, as I sat in the backseat on our way to the fair, "I went over to the midway. It surprised me the stuff I won. It was easy."

"Can you win me a panda?" I asked with urgent enthusiasm. "Can you? Can you?"

"Sure, I think so. Let's give it a try," Stan said with a blustery confidence that made me feel he was a pirate and I'd found my way into a chapter of *Treasure Island*. The only hurdle to get over to make my plan work, was my tight-fisted father fronting the twenty-five cents for each of the three throws we would need. Dad told stories all the time, lecturing, "I grew up in the Depression. I didn't have anything. I don't want to waste money. We had to leave the spare tire at the service station to get a tank of gas until we had enough to buy it back." I needed to hang him upside down by the ankles to get spare change from him, and sometimes I resorted to checking the pockets of his coats hanging in the closet for nickels and dimes. Fortunately, my dad seemed to want to make a good impression on Stan, and he agreed to fund this adventure.

At the fair, we headed over to the avenue with the noisy arcades, aiming for the one with the large stuffed pandas. They looked particularly engrossing, cute and huggable that day; the prospect of owning one fueled my hopeful enthusiasm. What if Stan wasn't up to the task this particular afternoon and missed all his shots? Could he win before my father stopped funding his 25-cent tries? All sorts of kids, sometimes even their parents, threw baseball after baseball at the stacked-up metal milk bottles, getting nowhere. They'd miss entirely or maybe just move them around.

Stan grabbed the first baseball, eyed the stack of weighted metal milk bottles standing in a small pyramid. He reared back, threw, and nailed the first stack. Next to him, another player tossed their ball and missed. Stan's second pitch easily annihilated that stack. With a casual confidence, the incredible Stan wound up again and sent the ball dead center. The bottles flew all over the place.

The man gave Stan that don't-come-back-here look, but Stan returned an easy smile. He struck down four more of these groups of bottles until the man made a show of "Look, a winner! A winner! You can win too! Come on, let's play!"

I jubilantly picked a black-and-white panda—and here's where the cello comes in. When I wrapped myself around the stuffed panda, I felt an inordinate sense of joy. Joy and comfort and security that I had a friend forever. I loved that stuffed animal with the big round eyes with black dots for pupils. At times, when I get the rich tone from the cello, from the resonating body of the instrument, there's a pleasing memory from when I was a little kid. As though I'm wrapped around the cello the same way I wrapped myself around my panda back then. There's a sense of acceptance, an enriching experience that transcends anything else that's going on with the world.

"You're Stan the Panda Man," I proclaimed. That's what I called Stan whenever I saw him. "Stan the Panda Man."

Chapter 26
Portland Cello Project

The Portland Cello Project is a musical group, as you would suspect, full of the magic of cellos. When this energetic ensemble performs, it is typically composed of six cellos and a couple other instruments, which may include a trumpet, percussion, keyboards, trombone, and a singer. This varies as cellists come and go to accommodate their schedules, including playing with other groups and the needs of the music being performed. The Portland Cello Project additionally adds other instruments for particular performances to reimagine the music selected.

As the Portland Cello Project states in its history:

> Under the artistic direction of Douglas Jenkins, the group grew and evolved a repertoire of over 1,700 pieces of music ... Jenkins developed a three-part philosophy for the group that has mostly remained its unchanged north star over the years:
> 1: To bring the cello places you wouldn't normally see it.
> 2: To perform music on the cello you wouldn't normally associate with the instrument.
> 3: To build bridges between different musical communities through collaborations and community outreach.

Recently, a new theater opened in suburban Beaverton, Oregon, on the west side of the hills separating it from downtown Portland. That's the end of town where Nike, Columbia Sportswear, and other sports apparel giants are situated.

The Patricia Reser Center is a 550-seat facility, a convenient size for dance company performances, bands, chamber ensembles, cabaret, theatre, lectures, and a whole raft of events that get lost in the cavernous auditoriums catering to Broadway touring companies. The Reser design is clean and modern, the layout contemporary with good sightlines and acoustics. But the main thing is it isn't too big.

The performance I attended featured music from the '90s. That is, the 1790s, 1890s, and 1990s. The Portland Cello Project ensemble included five cellists this evening, three of whom sat in standard chairs, as you'd expect. The other two were perched on stools, raising them a head higher than everyone else. To accommodate the height they were sitting, their cellos were held up into the air with extra-long endpins.

Firing up five cellos as the center of the ensemble, then adding select instruments, provides plenty of room to reimagine what the cello is capable of. All of this is broadly called *chamber music*. Before I started to investigate, I'd thought of chamber music as a harpsichord and violin played in an ornate room filled with dusty tapestries by musicians wearing powdered wigs. Wasn't chamber music a stuffy thing from long ago?

That is not the case. Chamber music is two or more musicians playing together. A chamber ensemble can be composed of any musicians of any type. When I lived in Minnesota, I had season tickets for the Saint Paul Chamber Orchestra. This was a small orchestra that filled much of the stage, but was smaller by far than their crosstown rivals, the Minnesota Orchestra, which had double and triple the number of instruments in every section.

The names "symphony" and "philharmonic" are interchangeable, according to several sources. Whichever name you given to these groups, they are large enough—with one hundred or so members—to play a complete score with all the instruments. Sometimes a city will have both a symphony and an orchestra, so these names help differentiate between them, even though there may not be much difference in the types of instruments the musicians play or the type of music they program. The word *philharmonic* means "music loving." It's based on the Greek root *phílos*—loving—and *harmonía,* meaning music.

When a group of musicians is called a "project," it takes you in another direction. The cellists in the Portland Cello Project present unexpected turns with sing-along sections, spotlighting soloists and playing compositions from their own members, which surprise audiences. I keep an eye out for their shows, but they don't have a regular schedule. One year they performed a Christmas show to a full house, but the next year it was hard to find them. It is difficult to know when they are going to play next. I wish they offered more shows.

Chapter 27
Laramie

While I was searching for cello events, consortiums, and workshops, a notice for something interesting popped up when I looked with the term *cello festival*. I found a one-day cello festival posted, described as: "including master classes, performances by celebrated professional cellists, plus participation in a cello chorus."

What is a cello chorus? I wondered.

This sounded like it would have a good punch to it, offered a variety of activities, and could be just what I was looking for. A photo from the preceding year's festival showed an entire stage full of cellos, an ocean of at least one hundred cellists awash across the stage. All the performers wore black shirts with a variety of pants and shorts. No surprise, since the event was located on a college campus.

The location? It was not a warm, sunny place to escape to in late winter. The cello festival would be held in Laramie, Wyoming.

There are cellos in Wyoming?

How is this possible? Wyoming doesn't have a lot of people to begin with. How many Wyomingites had any familiarity with any instrument other than a few guitars scattered across the prairie to accompany "Don't Fence Me In."

For starters, how would a beginner cellist like myself get to Laramie from Portland, or from anywhere for that matter? Is this something I could drive to? I saw the notice just two weeks before the festival, so there wasn't much time to plan. Turns out the driving distance exceeded one thousand miles. Could I fly inexpensively? But to where? Laramie certainly has an airport—but how big a plane could land there?

I contacted the cello festival's artistic director, Dr. Beth Vanderborgh, who is a professor at the University of Wyoming, where the festival is held. She replied with an exuberant invitation to attend, even promising me a loaner cello to play in the cello choir. "Please attend!"

"I can barely get through scales, so playing with a group is out of the question," I protested.

Dr. Vanderborgh insisted I participate. When I described my new-to-cello status, she sent me the Intermediate 4 music, the easiest parts they had.

There were ten tunes involved in the performance, all mercifully short. I printed and practiced each piece the best I could, though, I wasn't sure what the melodies were until we played them as a group because my part was entirely the baseline.

I used frequent flyer miles to get to Denver, then drove to Cheyenne in a rental car, turned left, and after a while, the road rose into the mountains into a sleet storm. The trip finished by gliding down a great, long hill into the historic Western town of Laramie.

The main attraction in this famous Wild West outpost is the University of Wyoming campus. Otherwise, there are a few attractions left over from more rustic times, mainly the old Territorial Prison which opened in 1872. Butch Cassidy, who was convict number 187, found lodging there for stealing horses. After a two-year stay in the 1890s, Butch organized the Wild Bunch and rode off to team up with the Sundance Kid to achieve immortality.

I found the music building and introduced myself to the woman to whom everyone was asking questions.

"Oh, George! Welcome! I'm Beth." She held her arms up in surprise, the way rodeo riders do after lassoing a steer.

Beth Vanderborgh is a creative tornado, always on the move. She cuts an energetic figure in black slacks and shirt, moving from one activity to another. Beth arranged for me to pick up the practice cello she promised and familiarized me with the schedule and building layout. The expansive Buchanan Center was a rambling complex with flexible performance spaces connected by a common lobby space. This cavernous interior suits Wyoming winters, offering ample indoor space where students and audiences can move around, relax, and mingle for casual discussions.

"There's the concert this evening. Also, a master class you can sit in on right now." She directed me toward the small recital hall nearby. Two sets of double doors opened into a rectangular performance space, paneled in blond wood, with comfortable theatre seating in the center and individual chairs at the sides and back.

A master class was underway when I found a chair near the stage. I'd never seen a session like this, making me curious about how they were conducted. Simple enough, a cello student sat in a chair at center stage, while a senior cellist observed them playing for a few minutes.

Usually, the master conducting the session had a copy of the music to follow if they wished. Though I soon realized that experienced cello players, especially professionals at this level, know most cello pieces and could play them back from memory, having had most of them in their repertory from the days when they were students.

Around the back of this long, narrow performance space, several cello cases stood against the walls. Turns out, the longer you play the cello, the more apt you are to stand the case up to take your cello out vertically. This helps spot beginners, like me, who lay their cases flat on the ground and open them as if they're coffins. I watched the master class for two hours. All the while, students were taking instruments out or returning them to their cases, and they talked quietly at the back of the room.

Guy Johnston was the master cellist giving this class. He dressed elegantly in dark clothes, as folks from the East Coast so often do. Out West we're more apt to put on a down jacket and maybe a brightly colored rain jacket over that. Spending much of my life on the West Coast, where people aren't so proper, I noticed these formalities. He had one student cellist after another play five minutes, providing feedback as they went. Johnston was, at the time, an associate professor of cello at the Eastman School of Music, the famous music school of the University of Rochester. "Eat, Sleep, Music" is the school's unofficial motto.

The Eastman School was founded in 1921 in New York, with funding from George Eastman, founder of Kodak, at a time when camera film came in canisters and the company was churning out profits. He named the company Kodak because the word sounded like a camera shutter clicking. Both Kodak and the Eastman School of Music are in Rochester, New York—a place weatherwise, I've been told, where clouds go to die.

Guy Johnson listened to a petite female graduate student play her cello. She sounded good to me, exhibiting concentration with a serious expression. I'd seen her in the practice room downstairs where my loaner cello was stored. She looked determined to pull great music out of the instrument. Playing with gravity onstage for the master class, her head tipped down toward the music stand, intently reading every note as she played. A music-is-serious-business approach. Her concentration appeared intense and she delivered, what I thought, seemed to be a solid rendition of a classical cello piece.

"Have you been performing much?" Johnston asked. He spoke respectfully, directly, with an urbane British accent and the respectful demeanor of a professional who's spent a great deal of time on stage before an audience.

"Only a little," the player said.

"Think about the audience. You're a bit hidden." He moved her music stand to the side so the audience could see her and pushed it down to the level of her knees but not so far that she couldn't easily read the score. Isn't the point of going to a performance to see the musician as well as listen to them? Can't do that if they're hidden behind a stand, seemed to be the message. Next, Johnston asked if she might sit more upright and look up at the audience with a pleasant expression, as it would help make a connection with them and improve the overall performance.

The student cellist quickly adjusted, started over, this time looking up and smiling. Maybe smiling a little too broadly, beaming at the audience unnaturally, like her eyes were headlights shining at them. She held a broad smile this way for such a long time as she played, it started to look menacing.

Playing the cello is complicated. There's a lot to think about.

The next student cellist had different issues. Johnston felt he didn't sit up naturally, as if his posture had become skewed as he'd developed his cello skills. Johnston lifted a thick strand of hair from the top of his head, demonstrating to the young man how a cello player should feel suspended, then dropped into the chair.

"You want to sit erect, as if pulled up from the top of your head," Johnston explained.

The student corrected his posture.

Johnston watched him. "Almost. Stand up and sit back down."

The student complied—stood up holding his cello and sat back down.

"Again. Do that several times, thinking about how to keep your back straight. Pretend a string is pulling your head up and dropping you down." Johnson remained understated and unfailingly polite.

The student worked at this. Each time he stood up and sat down differently as he worked to rethink his posture.

I was surprised by how many comments were given about appearance or posture, rather than some nuance about the progression of the notes or intonation or something more obviously musical. In some cases, individual passages in the music performed were taken apart and examined. Just not as often as I had imagined.

Another student had not learned to keep her fingers down on the strings. All four fingers could be on a string at once, or at least they should be held near the fingerboard. She lifted up all her fingers all over the place in every direction when they weren't pressing down on a string. "You have flying fingers," someone said.

The longer I observed the interactions between a student cellist and the cello master, the more I learned what to look for. But that didn't make me particularly better at analyzing my own playing.

I'd been around the cello community long enough to glimpse a fascinating hierarchy within its ranks. This informal organization is based on how well you play. Having these levels of cello expertise isn't a bad thing, as an informal ranking ensures that better players are assigned solos and play the more difficult parts in ensembles.

Beginners, such as myself, are part of the roiling sea of struggling cellists trying to find our way. We're working to make string crossings smoother. Pick out notes with the absence of frets to guide us. Hoping that with enough practice we will magically locate the invisible spot where the note you want is on which string. I could scratch my way through a sheet music rendition of "I've Been Working on the Railroad" or other recognizable songs we would play in the cello chorus at the Laramie festival, so long as I could be drowned out by the rest of the group.

The UW Cello Festival is primarily a single-day Saturday event with some preliminary activities on Friday evening when one of the visiting guest artists gives a performance. On this occasion, Dr. Lawrence Stromberg, from the faculty of the University of Delaware, had to change his program at the last minute when his accompanist came down with Covid. We were at the tail end of the pandemic at that time. Nobody was wearing a mask anymore, though there were still cases popping up here and there.

As it turned out, Stromberg took center stage for his solo program on the day the World Health Organization declared the pandemic emergency over.

Instead of a conventional music stand holding his sheet music, Stromberg used a collapsible stand that sat low, perhaps only three feet from the floor, with an iPad in a matte black holder. This was mounted to the tripod that electronically displayed the musical score. A two-piece foot pedal advanced the page or backed it up when tapped.

A speaker was fitted to the front of Stromberg's stand. It was the size of half a grapefruit. This wasn't to amplify the sound of his cello, but to play recordings of people talking about their lives in the neighborhoods around the Delaware town where Stromberg lives. He explained his interest in the lesser-known neighborhoods of his community where he seldom went. This turned into a project documenting people, letting them tell their story for the record, and adding cello music to accompany their words.

First, he played a recording of individuals talking about their lives, their challenges, what their days were like. A cello piece inspired by this followed. This pattern continued until the last of these vignettes, when the cello played along with the recording so the voice and music merged. The performance was well received, with cellist Stromberg earning an extra curtain call.

Saturday morning, the University of Wyoming Cello Festival commenced at a leisurely nine o'clock. Bakery boxes of donuts were stacked on a table, bait for the busloads of teenagers from around Wyoming and northern Colorado flooding the lobby. Cello cases were scattered all over, everywhere—red ones beat up from travel, blue ones with stickers all over, cheap black ones, and expensive graphite cases that shined.

The festival officially had room for one hundred participants and was filled to capacity. This end of the lobby *corralled*—it was Wyoming, remember—middle and high school students and a few teachers, who were milling about, talking music, fidgeting, tuning their instruments, and awaiting instructions.

This *herd*—sorry—of people created an inordinately composed, low-key atmosphere among all the students, their teachers. All this caused me to wonder if cellos made people mellow. I couldn't imagine a room full of trumpet players acting this calmly. Fill the room with drummers, and turmoil would have ensued.

Being the oldest dude in the room, I was invisible to the students. While I always have felt and acted about sixteen, my hair is as white as a polar bear. I hoped I added an arty-grandpa vibe to the festivities. No fault of the Wyoming teens, who were polite and focused on spending an easy day playing the cello. They were the nicest group of teenagers I'd been around in a long time, leaving me wondering if their communal interest in the cello was at the heart of it. All teenagers should be given cellos. Think of the problems this would solve.

The music for the Intermediate 4 cello part seemed relatively easy and would have been easier to play, had I spent more time practicing or had Mary Ann help me digest it. At ten o'clock, the intermediates headed downstairs to a large rehearsal room, while the advanced cellists went to the large theater to practice their parts. The downstairs rehearsal space we entered presented a clutter of music stands and chairs. A piece of paper with my name on it assigned me to the audience side of the cello choir and paired me with an affable eighth-grader from Cheyenne named Jamison.

Our conductor was Robert Stahly, a cellist himself. Stahly was a long-time high school music teacher from northern Colorado studying for an advanced degree. He kept a carefully trimmed beard, a conductor's highly groomed look, punctuated by a discrete eyebrow stud. He interacted well with us. I wish I'd had him as my high school band teacher instead of Dennis.

Conductor Stahly took us slowly through the first piece. Occasionally, he paused to play a few notes on his own cello, pointing out alternate fingering I could not pick up fast enough to make any sense out of. It was enough for me to keep my bow moving in time with the music while hitting an occasional note at the right time and something close to the pitch.

Fortunately, the hailstorm of inability I demonstrated when attempting to play along with the cello choir was assuaged by my new colleague. Jamison had been through the music with his teacher in preparation for this. He clued me in when I got lost. One familiar piece was "Dona Nobis Pacem," an often-performed round with overlapping repeated sections. I, of course, had not been through the music with a class and didn't know the terrain we were traversing. It went like this: The first intermediates played through the theme, then the seconds joined in; the thirds were next, followed at last by us, the fourth intermediates, taking up the rear. Regrettably, I hadn't been told that, due to starting last, we skipped the first half of the music and started in the middle.

This left me wandering astray. Starting too early. Playing with the wrong section. Bowing my cello long after everyone else had quit. All the other cello players finished, while it looked to me as though we had another half page of music to go. Jamison politely straightened me out on that, plus explained how the repeats worked on another.

"How long have you been playing?" Jamison asked.

"Six months," I said.

"You're pretty good for such a short time," said he. This encouraged me, though I quickly learned how to mime—playing without making a sound—when I got totally lost.

Once we'd gone over the music, we carried our cellos along a backstage corridor to the concert hall, where we joined the better cellists. The chairs behind these players were ours, and in the picture of our combined cello choir, I can be identified by my snow-colored hair rising from way in the back row, like a cumulus cloud on the distant Wyoming horizon.

From the stage, the audience seating looked like it went straight up into the sky. The rake to the auditorium was as steep as a mountainside. The conductor for the combined cello choirs was an old pro, Douglas Moore, who lived an hour or so south of Laramie. Moore was a grand, Zeus-like figure who taught music for years at Williams College before moving West. He's active in the extended regional music community and runs a website that makes sheet music easily available.

Moore is a nice man and talented musician. He sports a full head of hair and a bolt-of-lightning beard, making him an effective presence on the podium.

We started at once to play through all the combined cello choir songs without any preparation. Moore raised his baton without any warning—not even mentioning the name of the piece—gave the downbeat, and we began playing. *Bang.* All these cellos were playing at once, just like that. I'd never played with another cello player, much less more than one hundred of them.

We started with Mozart, "The Priests' Chorus from the Magic Flute," not a catchy tune, though recognizable and a challenge. The rest of the rehearsal went along with the same momentum. We were expected to know whatever tune came next without any mention of it, just belt it at the first flick of the conductor's baton. Jamison kept me organized.

Our cello choir worked through all the pieces, meaning we would be ready to perform later in the afternoon after one quick run through. After the rehearsal, we returned upstairs to be greeted by the box lunches promised in our registration fee. This being Wyoming, I hoped for American buffalo or bison, or beef brisket smoked with sage—something indigenous—but got the more orthodox assortment of potato chips augmenting a white bread ham-and-cheese sandwich.

During lunch, two viola da gambas were set out on the stage of the recital hall for us to play. This was advertised as "the Viola da Gamba Petting Zoo." Anyone who wanted to could give the gamba a try.

Gambas are predecessors to the cello. They look like a short cello with a big bottom and a small top that comes to a point. Six strings run down a wide fingerboard that is fretted like a guitar. There is no endpin to hold the body of the gamba high enough to play, so the instrument has to be squeezed between your calves to keep it afloat. A gymnast move.

I gave the gamba a try, held it between my knees or lower legs or wherever the instrument would stay put. My feet had to stay together to keep the gamba off the ground. When Beth came by to explain, she said, "You get used to holding the gamba with your gams."

The Gamba is an awkward thing, requiring a lot of effort to hold in place. Once you get stabilization figured out, you have to play it on top of that. The sound the gamba produces is of another era. It has the rustic, Renaissance air of hand-woven tapestries, knights in armor, and plays by Marlowe. I plucked the strings, then took a bow to them. The bow is held underhanded, rather than the grasping-the-top-of-the-frog method used on a cello.

Playing the gamba, makes it easier to understand why so many urgent developments came along to nudge this musical device's awkwardness toward the larger, rounder, more elegant cello we have today. Reducing the number of strings to a mere four simplified fingering. Adding an endpin to hold the cello aloft made the instrument hover at your knees, though endpins must have seemed experimental and controversial at the time they were first tried.

There are people who play the gamba today for their own amusement or in period music ensembles. I will never be one of them.

One other thing became clear to me in Laramie. Cello players are mellow and easy to get along with. They are a compact group of hobbyists and professionals drawn to the instrument. I felt I could include myself in this group after only a short time taking lessons. If you were to begin the cello today, you would be automatically absorbed into this universe. Many cellists first crossed paths as students or when playing in musical ensembles and remain in touch. They watch and listen to one another playing concerts everywhere the cello is bowed or its strings plucked. They seek each other out. Many meet and stay friends for a lifetime. I have never been welcomed into so friendly a place as this cello world.

These worldwide cello connections bring great talent to Laramie. One of these was Professor Leslie Jones, who journeyed all the way from the American College of Greece to perform and give a master class for adult learners.

Leslie conducted her master class casually. Each cellist played a selection under her gaze and received useful feedback. She usually focused on one aspect of the individual's performance, as this helped the student focus on that area of their playing rather than trying to work on too many things at once. Her approach was conversational and her comments easy to work with.

A pianist accompanied each cellist during this master class. Dr. Soyeon Kang, a collaborative pianist, performed with each cellist as if they'd practiced together in advance. Kang's ability to enhance the student's playing is a testament to her skill at sight reading and understanding how to work with another performer.

The term *accompanist* is familiar, though I now know how a *collaborative* pianist is different. Term *accompanist* was thought to imply secondary work, while the term *collaborative* pianist better represents the partnership with other musicians that is formed when they play together. Working with any mix of dancers, musicians, solo musicians, or other artists to enhance their performance is the collaborative pianist's skill.

The pianist subtly demonstrated her capabilities as a collaborator with one of the students in particular. This cellist, a man in his thirties, had not brought the piano accompaniment to the piece he performed. He went ahead and played, with Leslie making suggestions and the cellist trying to add them to different sections.

While he struggled with all this, Kang deftly searched an iPad where she stored and displayed her music, found the piece he was playing, and started playing the piano part as the cellist played. The marvel of digital information storage and acuity of an alert collaborative pianist enhanced the cello experience.

All of a sudden, the master classes were over, and we went from milling around to changing into black shirts and heading downstairs to perform our hour-long concert. My hands were shaking.

We intermediates would perform our pieces first. Then we'd abandon the stage so the advanced cellists could perform their tunes, while we huddled in the passageway or snuck out into the auditorium to listen.

For the grand finale, the intermediates would join these better players, and together our combined cello choirs would play pieces by Bach, Goltherman, and Bodi. The last piece we all looked forward to would be "I've Been Working on the Railroad."

To begin the concert, we simply ambled on stage with stumbling resolve. Around fifty cellists made up the intermediate choir. I was by far the oldest with the average age of my colleagues being around sixteen. I was at least twenty years older than the next adult beginner, though I was also the newest and felt I mercilessly stood out in every way I could. A great wave of desperation overcame me when I discovered my assigned seat stuck me at the edge of the stage. Right in front of the audience, out where everybody could see each detail of my glaring foolishness. My trusty eighth-grader sat next to me, with the conductor right in front of us.

A giant imaginary arrow pointed at me, saying, "He doesn't know what he's doing!"

I tried to hold my borrowed cello casually, as if prepared for a major concert. Jamison and I organized our music on the stand and checked with other players to make sure we had the music in order.

A problem for me in rehearsal had been that the endpin on the bottom of my loaner cello didn't have a rubber stopper. Without this traction, the pin slipped.

Earlier, Douglas Moore, the conductor, suggested I use my belt to hold the endpin in place. This sounded like a good fix, so I intended to take my belt off once I sat down to do this. I'd route the leather through the buckle around a chair leg, then stab the point at the bottom end rod into the leather. Now, though, I felt concerned that if I took off my belt, it might look amiss in front of an audience of parents on one side and a slew of young musicians on the other, so I stopped. Fortunately, Jamison rescued me from that misadventure and offered the endpin strap he brought since he had a rubber tip on his cello that did not slip.

No sooner did I sort all that out, calm down, and brace myself for the baton to come down when my next humiliation tied up at the dock. A mom, dad, and a younger brother sat down in the seats right in the front row, facing me like we were a TV set playing their favorite program. They were inches away.

"You all ready?" the mom asked.

"Yeah," Jamison replied.

"Oh, great," I thought.

"Are you his parents?" I inquired.

"Yes, we are," the mom said proudly.

"Jamison's been getting me through this. He's been very helpful," I told them.

"Isn't he great?" Mom said.

Our dapper intermediate group conductor, Robert Stahly, took the podium to applause. He bowed humbly. Festival director Dr. Beth Vanderborgh appeared with a microphone and welcomed everyone, celebrated the participants, and when finished, headed toward the back of the cellists onstage.

She'd told me previously that she joins the other teachers and some senior members of the advanced cellists behind the intermediates to "beef up their sound."

The place I really should have been sitting should have been behind the other cellists in back, where I wouldn't be easily seen or heard. Or maybe I could have hidden in the next room and not even come out on stage.

At that moment, I remembered how Beth had pushed me to participate—*just get out there and give it a try*. Once you try something and see how it goes, the next time you know what to expect—the time after that, the whole experience seems so simple.

Conductor Stahly gave the downbeat, beginning the first of our pieces, Handel's *Judas Maccabeus*. Daunting title. Our version was short, so we got through the piece without a hitch. I got lost on every song we played but fought my way back to where my colleagues were going and finished around the same time they did.

We played a short piece by Brahms next, then eventually "Dona Nobis Pacem," the round that caused me such grief in rehearsal. I did my best to look serious while moving the bow back and forth, changing fingers around the fingerboard while figuring out how to get back in sync with my fellow cellists.

Mercifully, the conductor finished conducting about the same time most of us stopped playing the last number, with me finding my way to the end shortly thereafter. We intermediates stood to receive friendly applause from parents and friends. We bowed by looking down at our shoes, as we'd been instructed to do. This is much smarter than bending over while holding a cello. We evacuated the stage as the advanced cello choir walked on. I don't know what they played, other than what songs the program listed, as we were offstage in a hallway during their set.

The intermediates headed back onstage to join in the combined cello choirs. This time we filled in the seats behind the advanced players. Mercifully I wound up in the back row, right where I should have been in the first place. Hidden from humanity.

Seated in obscurity, it became much easier to take in the full scope of the cello ensemble. Massive rows of seats climbed high in front of us as we looked up to the audience. The scale of the proscenium created a yawning opening to perform in.

More impressive yet were all these cellos together on stage. Individual players doing the best they could to make everyone sound better. The tones and attack of the different instruments coming in late, holding a note a little too long, the vibrations from the instruments connecting into a great unity as they played. Who'd have thought there were that many cellos in Wyoming?

We closed with "I've Been Working on the Railroad," featuring a wooden train whistle the conductor got to blow.

Laramie That Evening

After surviving the afternoon concert, the teenagers loaded onto their buses and headed back home. I returned my loaner cello to its locker, and lolled around for during the hour break before heading to the more intimate recital hall for the final Cello Festival Gala Concert.

This promised to be an evening event for those participants who stayed and members of the greater Laramie community. When the doors opened, I once more grabbed a chair as close to the stage as I could.

Sitting near the performers provided a great opportunity to study the techniques of accomplished cellists. How close they keep their fingers to the fingerboard when they play. How they economize moving from one note to another, especially during string crossings. Methods to use the string you're on to play the next note, rather than jumping to another string.

The first piece of this evening's performance was by Gwyneth Walker, titled "About Trains" for six cellos. The performers were an all-star cast of Beth Vanderborgh, the artistic director; Lawrence Stromberg, visiting from the University of Delaware; Leslie Jones, the professor from Greece; and Stephanie Flores, Mitchell Smith, and Jason Cox from the school's music program.

Having six cellos playing together without any other instruments was still new to me. Especially interesting was how different parts of the music moved from one cellist to another, sometimes in a surprising order. The momentum bounced from one player to another. One plucked a note, then another bowed the melody. This went back and forth across the six cellists onstage in a lively fashion, sounding country western and ending with all the cellists shouting "Yippee!"

The performance that followed featured Guy Johnston, guest cellist from the Eastman School of Music, with collaborative pianist Chi-Chen Wu, performing the *Cello Sonata in G minor, op. 19: III. Andante* by Sergei Rachmaninoff. I knew nothing about Rachmaninoff, including how to spell his name without looking it up.

During the short intermission following the first cello ensemble, a lone stage manager cleared the six-chair setup, replacing it with a single chair and music stand. That done, he pushed a grand piano onto the stage by himself. The piano sailed into view, resembling a massive ocean liner pulling into port.

I have a smidge of familiarity with Steinway pianos. Even owned a small professional upright Steinway in my piano lesson days. Mine fit against my living room wall. I even managed to orchestrate a tour of the Steinway factory, making the arrangements through the piano store I dealt with when living in Minnesota.

Steinway had made pianos in Astoria, Queens, New York, since the 1870s. My appointment was in the morning so I could continue from there to LaGuardia and fly home. The Steinway operation left quite an impression, forty years ago, as I'm recalling the tour today.

The notable thing I saw when I pulled up to the factory was the Steinway lumberyard. Carefully selected wood was stored outdoors in the weather. Stacks upon stacks of lumber—big, long pieces—rested in roughly sawed piles subjected to hot, humid summers and snowy winters.

Wood continues to live long after it's cut because it incessantly absorbs and loses moisture, bends or resists bending, reacts to temperature changes, moves around, shrinks, and expands.

When the wood is selected to be made into a piano, the lumber is cut and formed with a lot of time devoted to allowing the parts to sit and age. This lets the joined pieces become accustomed to one another.

The outside rim of a grand piano is made up of multiple layers of wood, bent and glued into shape. Then it is left to stand and age some more since bending adds a lot of tension to the wood, and it needs time to adjust. There was an impressive room at the Steinway factory full of these stately outer wooden rims of pianos standing like sculptures, resting.

The stupendously long Steinway rolling onstage in Laramie embodied all this know-how.

The basic Steinway sizes are: Model S for Small, Model M for Medium, Model L for Large, and Model B for Big. The colossal piano docking on the Laramie stage now was a Model D, which stands for *Damn Big*. Eight feet, ten and three-quarter inches long; four feet, six inches wide; and weighing nearly one thousand pounds. Lie down on the floor and think about how much bigger that is than you. The design was first introduced in 1884. At least one of these lives in Laramie.

We watched as an elegant stage picture was created for Guy Johnston's performance: the artistic lines of the Steinway with a single chair in front for the cellist and a music stand positioned slightly to the side of the chair.

Applause warmed the hall as Guy Johnston carried out his cello, with pianist Chi-Chen Wu walking alongside him. They formally acknowledged the audience and took their seats. Johnston wore a dark suit and Wu a concert dress.

Johnston gave a fine-tuning screw a final adjustment—then let his left hand dangle, shaking it out like a pitcher preparing to throw a World Series game. When ready, he looked over his shoulder to the pianist, giving an invisible signal to begin. Johnston was immediately all over his cello with a complete mastery of how to coax sound from it. He plucked and pulled and bowed and rocked, realigning with the instrument as he played with athletic flourish.

Rachmaninoff takes a lot out of the cellist, audience, collaborative pianist, everybody. His work is described as full of expressiveness, song-like melodicism, with dense counterpoint textures with rich orchestral colors. To me, the composer creates a wall of sound with a lot of by hurling the music around, carrying the theme forward and focusing your attention. Johnston's amazing performance went on for the better part of an hour, with precise synchronization between him and his pianist.

What a great lesson watching him play. Sitting so close, I caught nuances in his technique, such as Johnston preparing for a clean attack on a note by resting the bow on a string, then digging the horsehair in so it made a strong, clean start at the beginning of the note. Mary Ann had taught me this technique, but I'd never seen it done with such skill.

At my next lesson, I went over the experience of performing on a cello in Laramie with Mary Ann, and in particular explained my angst at being on stage without the ability to play the music.

"Now you have that experience. You'll remember it. Your first performance with a group of musicians," Mary Ann said.

"I felt like I was an imposter," I said.

"That's all part of the learning process. We have all gone through this," she said.

Chapter 28
Search for a Strad

Now that I'd played some better cellos, my resolve to find a Strad and play "Here Comes the Sun" grew more focused. I'd been practicing the tune during my regular lessons and had enough of it memorized to focus on getting this done.

When I'd spoken with Kenneth Slowik at the Smithsonian Chamber Orchestra months before to talk cello, he indicated that July might work for a visit. In June, he was booked with the Oberlin Music programs and other events. Oberlin has some of the premier teaching conferences for young musicians anywhere. They run an iconic operation, attracting top-tier teachers, professionals, and musicians who want more experience in an encouraging setting.

I'd come a long way since then in my playing ability.

When I asked to set a specific day to meet in July, Slowik deferred, saying we could try to set something up closer to the date. I felt good about this exchange. Kenneth Slowik is enthusiastic about cellos and possesses an ocean of knowledge about the history of string instruments, orchestras, and luthiers. He was also brimming with what's happening currently in music and seems to know, and has played with, every notable cellist, musician, and conductor on earth.

I waited weeks until we were well into summer before attempting to set up that July meeting in Washington, D.C. When I had to make flight reservations, I sent an email asking for a date in the middle of July to plan this visit.

No response.

I went ahead and booked the tickets but waited a while before sending another email. Didn't get a response after trying again, so I called his office. A recording said to leave a message along with the date you were leaving it. This indicated messages weren't checked often. I figured that Slowik's calendar was filled.

That June, Susan and I took a three-week trip to visit friends and family in Scandinavia, during which time I didn't follow up. We had met a Norwegian couple, Marit and Gjert, on our Camino hike and discovered that Marit and I shared the same birth year, month, and date. We calculated that we were born four hours apart, Marit in Oslo and me in San Diego.

We decided to celebrate our next birthday in Norway and sailed in their boat to a cabin on a small island off the southern coast. Gjert served moose stew, spatchcocked chicken, and grilled reindeer. They were great hosts.

Upon our return home, I left another message for Slowik at the Smithsonian. I didn't overdo reaching out, but why waste a trip to the East Coast only to stand outside the building, wondering if I should have been more unwearyingly assertive?

When I described the situation to a sympathetic friend, he assured me the person I was trying to see had clearly demonstrated a helpful willingness before.

"You just haven't bubbled up to the top of his to-do list quite yet," my friend Derby assured me.

My heart sunk thinking about missing the chance to see a Stradivarius up close. This sent me on a hunt for a Strad in a different museum, just in case the D.C. visit fell through.

I was surprised to learn of a major instrument museum in Phoenix, Arizona. Phoenix, with its blast-furnace summers incinerating the parched landscape, didn't suggest musical instruments to me any more than Laramie had suggested cellos.

When I looked up Phoenix museums, I found the Arizona Science Center right away. One of the science exhibits allows the visitor to stuff a giant nose with balls to watch how a sneeze works. If there were no Strads in Phoenix, I could always head over to the nose and watch the sneeze.

Turned out, the Musical Instrument Museum in Phoenix, which refers to itself as MIM, claims to house the largest collection in the world. They call themselves "The World's Only Global Musical Instrument Museum."

After some effort, I connected with Matthew Zeller, curator of Europe at MIM, who replied, "We actually do not have many cellos in our collection, only a handful of old German and Bohemian instruments. Hopefully, over the course of the next few years, I should be able to acquire some new examples for us."

High-end instruments such as Strads and those from his fellow Cremona luthiers are astronomically expensive. There are a limited number to go around, so it's a challenge for any museum to obtain one. Zeller also made the important observation that these historic cellos have become works of art. As a result, the prices don't reflect those of an instrument that is played, but instead something to look at and admire, without hearing what it sounds like.

I asked Zeller why we can't duplicate Stradivarius instruments. He responded that luthiers can make very fine violins and cellos today. The difference is that the old instruments carry a certain aesthetic value that is attained over time. That doesn't mean they are always better, but the reality is that most Strads are exquisite instruments. We can't duplicate any instrument exactly. Each instrument will always be its own. The challenge is to make each one the best it can be, the best version of itself.

I looked further, finding the National Instrument Museum in Vermillion, South Dakota, located on the University of South Dakota's campus.

I queried the museum, and Arian Sheets, curator of stringed instruments, got right back to me, writing, "We don't currently have instruments that are set up for regular playing, but I can show you examples that interest you."

If I couldn't play the instrument, that really missed the point of chasing it down, didn't it? Where else might a Stradivarius cello be found?

With just a week to go before my trip, I brought up by dilemma with Mary Ann at my lesson. Obliging as usual, she shifted in her chair and ran a hand through her thick white hair as I situated myself with my cello. After giving this some thought, Mary Ann said she couldn't think of another institution with a Strad cello readily available, other than what she'd already shared.

In July, I began my trip back east with a continent-hopping flight to New York City, then couch surfed with my charming friend Cyndy up the Hudson in Tarrytown. In the morning, I rode the train into the city. From Grand Central Station I hiked up Fifth Avenue, passing between the glass-cubed Apple Store and Plaza Hotel, wandering north along the park to the Metropolitan Museum of Art.

I had made a sustained effort for months to get in touch with one of the Met curators about their instrument collection—particularly, their cellos—without getting a whiff of a response. I emailed the Met several times, leaving messages that went unanswered. Multiple emails and phone messages with no response from a soul in any of the several departments I tried, including media relations and others in this huge museum.

With no response whatsoever from the Met's musical instrument department, I figured I would simply go visit them anyway. Maybe I'd run into a curator lingering in the instrument collection I could talk with about cellos. Odder things have happened. Why not throw myself into the path of opportunity?

I clambered the monumental steps to the museum on a sultry July day and found my way into the lobby, where I purchased an admission ticket. I'd explored the Met many times over the years, but the layout seemed to get progressively more complicated each time I visited.

A uniformed guard told me where the instruments were displayed. Upstairs was the answer. At the top of the stone stairs, I asked another person in museum attire for the instruments once more. They thought for a minute before describing a route a lost hobbit might take to burrow down through tree roots, follow a trail up a marshy glen, over rocks and gullies, to find a beehive full of honey—oh stop. He said to go through the Japanese art area.

Inside this exhibit, I wound around in a loop but popped out where I had started. When I asked a different guard for help, he said, "Go back there."

The guy pointed from whence I came.

Once again, I wound my way around the Japanese displays, wondering why no one else was in here. No guards were stationed inside.

I continued past the painted screens and mats to what seemed to the back wall. Looked and looked. Forced myself around the farthest edge of the last partition. Took another step, and there, tucked in the deepest reaches of an alcove, was a pair of hidden doors.

No signs pointed these out. A flicker of light did not illuminate them.

I walked through the hidden doors, coming into a bright, pleasant area with plenty of signs guiding me toward the musical instrument collection. I entered the space. Inside stretched a long, narrow instrument room. Individual instruments were housed in large plastic boxes—reminding me of the glass box of the Apple Store entrance a few blocks toward Midtown.

An enormous saxophone, a great python of an instrument over six feet tall, stood in a box near the doors on the side of the room. There were scads of other curious and familiar music-making items through the space.

And there was what I'd been searching for. A particularly svelte cello with clean, classic lines appeared to float in the air. The silhouette of the instrument seemed perfectly proportioned. A human form. The figure of a woman with C-bouts for a waist, rounded on the top and bottom. A bikini would have looked great on it—fit perfectly. Turned heads. Drawn crowds to see this spectacular cello, which seemed suspended in midair. Yes, this cello had left the joyous world of music and descended into the world of art.

The cello on display in the Plexiglas case was made in Cremona, Italy, in 1714. Think about what else was happening in the world at that time. It would be another nine years before a young Benjamin Franklin left Boston for Philadelphia to begin his patriotic career. The Copernican theory of the universe, placing planets in orbit of the sun, was not fully accepted when the trees were felled and seasoned so they could be fashioned into this instrument.

There was the Batta-Piatigorsky cello, named for the two cellists who played it: Alexandre Batta (1816–1902), who was Dutch, and Russian-born Gregor Piatigorsky (1903–1976).

Advances in string design meant cellos could be made smaller and still produce great sound. This allowed Antonio Stradivari to design this smaller instrument, making the cello easier to play. The instrument I was looking at was a Stradivarius Forma B. It is slightly smaller than the popular cellos made before it and became the standard all cellos since are compared to.

The Batta-Piatigorsky cello in the Met is considered the best specimen of the Forma B cello in existence. It was no longer an instrument that made music, but instead sunk into a state of priceless art.

I admired this item. The Strad was gorgeous. The proportions stunning. Easy on the eyes.

I yearned to hear it play. At least to hear the sound it makes. With such an important specimen of Stradivari cello craftsmanship, would there be a way to listen? There must be a recording? Is this Strad ever placed in the hands of a cello master? Are there other cellos in the Met collection? There was no other information about this in the display room and no one to ask. I'm sure that even if there were a person available, their response would be little more than the oft heard, mindless response, "Check on our website." I had already done this.

There is great beauty in seeing cellos and violins and violas as sculptures. Many other exotic instruments were on display in the Met instrument collection that day. Horns with tubing all wrapped around the bell to make them more compact. All sorts of brass and woodwinds. In an adjoining room, a towering display of horns looked dramatic.

There was some music playing, but it could hardly be heard. A couple small screens placed at ankle height played recordings of a symphony in black and white as I walked by. They were positioned near the floor, it seemed, to avoid being noticed.

I was meeting my friend Scott Sandell at the museum for lunch. I've known Scott for fifty years, since we worked in the Walker Art Center together in our youth. If I could talk him into it, couldn't we lift the plastic case off the Strad long enough for me to belt out "Here Comes the Sun" before anyone noticed. I could convince him we would get away with it.

Scott's an artist, I figured he'd understand.

After I lurked with musical instruments waiting a while, Scott arrived a little late. I met him in the lobby and he steered me to the building's basement cafeteria where school kids eat with their teachers during field trips. Usually, we find a more cosmopolitan aboveground restaurant with windows, sunlight, cocktails, views of the trees and people walking by, but this is where he wanted to eat today.

He preferred eating at MoMA. "They have great potato chips," he said.

The sub-basement cafeteria had a ceiling low enough that I instinctively ducked when I entered. School-aged kids fidgeted around us. We ordered food that had sat in a steamer to keep it warm. As I bit into the soft, damp cheeseburger wrapped in foil and the cold French fries, I thought of artier places to dine. Places where they let you hear the cellos play. MoMA, where the potato chips are fresh—a place where, if they had a cello, they'd let me play it. Surely they would. I should have listened to Scott and met him there.

I told him about the cello I'd seen, but not heard, and how uninhabited and lifeless and non-musical the experience was. "Where was the music in the musical instruments?" I asked.

He listened to me go on about the number of times I'd tried to contact the Met staff without a single response and my sense of being dismissed. My experience with the music department felt flat as the taste of a soft, damp cheeseburger.

On the eve of heading down to Penn Station to catch that train to D.C., I sent a Hail Mary email to Kenneth Slowik, who had not replied to my carefully timed emails and ultra-polite phone messages asking for the meeting we'd discussed months before.

It would be my last attempt to see him to talk cellos and see his instruments if they were on display. In this last email, I asked to meet him at noon on Friday, which is often the easiest day to find time on someone's calendar. I sent this, certain my request would disappear, unseen.

My phone rang within a minute.

"Can we meet on Thursday at eleven o'clock instead?" Slowik asked, without having to say, "You certainly are persistent."

"Of course," I replied, knowing I'd have to change a lunch date and rearrange the entire visit—which seemed like a minor inconvenience. "Where shall we meet?"

"Call me from the lobby when you arrive," Slowik said.

"The lobby of what?" I asked.

"The National Museum of American History."

I had not felt this level of jubilation and refreshment since—let me think—I first sipped Tanqueray gin and Schweppes tonic on ice with a slice of lime on a hot summer day, or spread cream cheese on a darkly toasted, boiled and baked bagel and took a chewy bite.

In D.C., I couch-surfed with Joey. He'd just bought a new couch, and I'd encouraged him to get one long enough for a six-foot-one-inch visitor to stretch out on. The couch was located under his living room windows, where a lightning storm treated me to a deluge and fireworks show the first night.

In the morning, we took the Metro over to the National Mall and walked along the vast expanse until we reached the museum. Inside the lobby, a geodesic dome covered the space. When you stand in it, to the right is a horse-drawn wagon. To the left sits a twelve-ton marble statue of George Washington. How many buildings have floors capable of holding that much weight? In this representation of President Washington, the father of our country is arranged as an Olympian Zeus figure. He wears a toga and is bare chested with sandals on his gigantic feet. Washington holds a sword in one hand and points skyward with the other.

Washington's eyes seemed to follow me around the lobby, as if he were about to say, "You don't know how to play the cello well enough to be here."

A few minutes before our appointment, I called Slowik as planned. He instructed me to turn right at Washington, go up the escalators, and take another turn.

Kenneth Slowik wore a dark suit without a tie on this hot, humid day. His curly hair looked artistic and academic. He greeted Joey and me with a welcoming smile and a naturally pleasant demeanor. I began to relax a little.

A display case filled the entryway inside the first set of doors to a small auditorium.

"This is a quartet of Amati instruments." Slowik indicated a cello, viola, and two violins in the case. "These are used for performances."

Here were old Cremona-made instruments that were both works of art and working instruments. Amati is considered by some the inventor of the violin. To see this compact collection all together like this felt unreal.

We continued into the auditorium, which was set up with chairs facing a modest stage. Slowik scooted a couple chairs around so we could talk.

"What would you like? To talk about cellos? Do you want to see some, too?" Slowik asked.

I told him, "I'd like to get as close to the cellos as I can."

When I first got that surprise call from Slowik months before, I did not know his background as a cellist or his achievements. I knew those now and melted a little when he mentioned that he'd performed the month before with Yo-Yo Ma right here on this stage. This performance took place when Ma was presented the Smithsonian Great Americans Medal. The award recognizes lifetime achievements, which for Ma included "His engaging audiences in unexpected, wide-ranging, and poignant explorations of music's lasting role in our culture," as was said that evening by the museum's Anthea M. Hartig.

Slowik was gracious. When I asked about cello chairs, I mentioned that when I watch videos of Yo-Yo Ma playing, he seems to be lying back, as if relaxed in a lounge chair.

Slowik didn't think so. He ran over to a storage closet to the side of the stage. Inside were folding tables and some rigid-looking classroom style chairs of no particular character. He located an extra-sturdy metal chair.

"Yo-Yo used this chair." Slowik pulled it from the closet and turned it upright for me to sit in if I wanted. Of course I did since Yo-Yo Ma had used it.

"I expected something more exotic." For weeks I'd been overthinking what cello chair would be best for me. I was imagining some sort of special chair that great cellists would use, but those evidently don't exist.

From there, he talked about playing styles and how they changed with instrument design. The way string technology advances led the way to allowing cellos to be made smaller. The era when cellos did not have an endpin, obliging performers grip the instruments with their legs when they played.

Another story involved a short-lived attempt to have women play the cello sidesaddle because it was considered more ladylike. I heard later from another source that strict nuns also insisted women play with the cello to the side at times.

Slowik mentioned the Woody Allen movie *Take the Money*, in which Allen's character tries to play cello in a marching band. To do this, he plays, scoots his chair up, falls behind, and tries to play the cello while sitting in the chair again and again as the band marches on without him.

I asked about the best ways to practice when you're as new as I am, compared to how a highly skilled player would rehearse.

Slowik told me how Yo-Yo Ma practices being in the moment. He works at that. He had obviously reached the level where his technique was in place after uncountable hours playing. Being in the moment was his way of playing his best.

"What about all these different endpins available?" I asked. "Some are made of unusual metals or graphite. Some are hollow or filled with a different material."

Slowik explained that some of the interest around exotic endpins came from the theory that because the endpin sits on the stage floor, the floor picks up the vibrations and amplifies the sound. This essentially makes the floor an extension of the instrument. He didn't feel that was the case, and cellos don't work this way.

This scuttled my idea that I needed a spendy replacement endpin that could run into the hundreds of dollars. My belief that Yo-Yo Ma used an exotic lounge chair also vanished. How refreshing to see these matters cleared up, especially if it meant I didn't need to buy something extra that didn't really make a difference. It was becoming cheaper and cheaper to play the cello by the minute.

Slowik checked his watch, his window of availability diminishing as he rose from his chair. "Would you like to see some instruments?"

Just that fast, we headed out of the auditorium, up into a secure realm within the museum. Here, administrative wheels turn, decisions are made, and the work is done to keep this part of the Smithsonian operation moving.

We badged through one door after another.

As we went, Slowik explained that the collection has more than five thousand instruments. Most are held offsite where they can be securely stored in a climate-controlled space. Only a handful of instruments, a small part of the Smithsonian's collection, can be stored in this building or any of their many other museums. There is just too much to keep in one place.

We reached a set of secure double doors, managed the security process again, and went inside a storage room stuffed full of musical instruments. The instruments stored here were used in exhibits or played by professional musicians during performances.

Two harpsichords occupied a huge amount of square footage. They were covered in what looked like custom-fitted moving quilts. One harpsichord was fourteen feet long. We didn't touch anything.

There were tall metal lockers in the style of a high school gym, except these were much larger, sturdier, and more secure. Holes in the metal doors ventilate some of the lockers and make it easier to find what you're looking for. In one of the cabinets, guitars filled the rack. Every type I'd ever seen. The next one stored violins. Everything carefully positioned and catalogued. There were trumpets, saxophones, some instruments in cases, others without. Everything had its own lock.

We went to a cabinet where several cellos rested, none of them in a case. Another lock on these doors.

Slowik took a dark brown cello out, turning the front to us. I had been around cellos enough by this point to see some of the differences among this collection. One cello came from a Midwestern luthier who made it around 150 years ago. Another had a similar story but bore a much darker finish and what appeared to be a huskier build—though that assessment might have come from its deep color rather than the actual size. Each instrument looked amazing in its own way.

Slowik mentioned how bigger cellos were sometimes cut down to a smaller size. This was done to make them easier to play as improvements in string technology became available. "Let me show you an example," Slowik said.

Inasmuch as most Stradivarius cellos have been cut down to make them more easily played, only three unaltered large-form cellos remain. These cellos are the Medici in the Istituto Cherubini of Florence, the 1699 Castelbarco in the Library of Congress, and the 1701 Servais at the Smithsonian.

I tried to keep up with Slowik's fast walk as we locked up the cellos, then snaked our way around the stuffed storage room. This took us around various musical obstacles, between lockers and boxes and small crates, to a rack of cello cases. No two cello cases matched. One had old-fashioned, squared-off corners. Another looked black and bulky. A modern graphite case stuck out as bright and shiny and lean.

Slowik selected one of the cello cases, stood the case up, and removed the instrument, which looked smaller than those we'd been looking at, though not by much.

"You can see how this was cut down. The curve of the top is different where it meets the edge."

Slowik had Joey and me feel where the arch on the cello's front came all the way over to the side in places, while in other parts the arch leveled out before reaching the edge.

"Is this ..." I began.

"Yes, of course," Slowik answered.

"Really?"

"Would you like to play it?" Slowik offered casually.

"Yes, of course." My spine tingled as it had the first time I'd watched *Rosemary's Baby.*

"Yes, this is a Stradivarius," Slowik said, handing it over. "Hold it a minute for me, would you? While I find a bow."

I carefully wrapped my fingers around the cello's neck. "Got it."

The level of responsibility weighed on me as I held one of the remaining sixty-three Stradivarius cellos on Earth. A blunder handling this instrument could turn into a sad headline, I worried. Slowik picked out a bow from an assortment locked inside a different cage. Then he gave the bow to me while he took back the cello. We returned to the other end of the room where there was some space.

Joey and I looked at each other in amazement. He'd been following along on all this, asking a question or two, and now nodding as I handed him my phone.

"Take a lot of pictures," I said.

"Roger that," Joey replied.

Slowik found space in the corner by the doors, where a couple of stray chairs were situated. A fire extinguisher, broom, and dustpan with a long handle cluttered the wall. Slowik, one of the premier cellists in the world, sat in the chair with the Stradivarius, relaxed and comfortable. Being one of the newest and worst cello players on Earth, I sat in awe, watching from the other chair.

With his level of experience, he deftly adjusted the tuning pegs. I'd have been afraid of breaking something if I had to do that. Once in tune, Slowik played a classical riff, stood up, and handed me the Stradivarius. "Give it a try?"

I took the instrument and stuck the point of the endpin into the edge of a linoleum floor tile. When I played a C scale, I went slowly, carefully placing my fingers on the wrong spots. Hitting notes off-key, moving up the scale and back down.

"God Save the King" came next. It's easy. Or at least it is back home. This was the simple tune Carlos had played for us when requested during his performance in Spain. I got through this song more easily than I could the scales, in part because Kenneth Slowik graciously let me play without making any comments.

"Would you like to compare that to the larger cello?" Slowik asked, standing over me.

"Yes, please. That would be great." I melted.

In a moment, Slowik appeared carrying the larger instrument. Darker hued. He showed us how the top had been constructed and some details about the instrument. Particularly interesting is how often these old instruments have been repaired, updated, and had parts replaced.

"Give me an A," Slowik said.

What pride I felt to play the A string on one Stradivarius to help tune another. I knew which string that was. Once he had this new instrument up and running, we traded our Stradivarius cellos. I never thought in my entire life I'd be able to write that sentence in a book.

This new instrument was larger. Heftier. I tried the scale again. Then "God Save the King" on this one too. I missed one note after another in my excitement. Uselessly tried to correct the pitch when I was off.

I looked to Kenneth Slowik, artistic director, master cellist, who played with Yo-Yo Ma. "I must be painful to watch," I said.

"I've seen everything." Slowik smiled broadly, leaving me feeling much better about myself than the quality of my playing would suggest.

He left for a moment to return the first cello to its case. As Mary Ann said early in our lessons, "If you see an opportunity, take it." I played "Here Comes the Sun" from memory.

I sounded distinguished and impressive as I delivered the tribute to George Harrison. At least it seemed that way to me.

The tune put me right back under the dashboard of my old Volvo with the Beatles, having just finished attaching my new tape deck and popping in the cassette of the new *Abbey Road* album, the year we landed on the moon.

"Try more pressure and a slower bow," Slowik said when he returned.

I slowed my bow across the G string while pushing harder with my index finger. The cello rumbled, exploded with sound. Produced resonance like a throbbing helicopter passing by. There was an earthiness, the way ginseng root smells when sliced, a thoroughbred breathing.

The cello rang long after I lifted the bow from the string, sounding the way Mary Ann had explained good tone: a big, juicy apple that explodes when you bite it.

What a memory.

I asked Kenneth Slowik if he would play something so I could listen. He produced that same stunning, out-of-this-world tone with each note. Gingerly played the scale I struggled with, then noodled around with some elegant, recognizable classical passages. I watched as he walked down the A string to reach the cello's highest notes, demonstrating how he positioned the bow close to the bridge to get the clearest note from the string.

When I played, he had mentioned how I should keep my fingers down. When I asked him to show me what I did wrong, he rotated his left hand up at the wrist, fingers off the fingerboard. This took them far from the strings, upping the chances of hitting the wrong spot on the wrong strings when I put them down again.

We ran out of time.

Of the sixty-three Stradivarius cellos in the world, I had just played two of them.

As Slowik started back to return the cello, I said, "Cellos have names."

"Yes."

"What was the first one?" I asked.

"The Marylebon," he said.

I gasped. "And which was this?"

"The Servais," he said.

Many people say this is the most beautiful-sounding cello in the world.

I believe this is true.

Chapter 29
Coda

This musical excursion began on a Camino de Santiago trek, the catalyst a performance by Carlos Ariel Gracia Baez, an altogether captivating cello player and lecturer. He had that Spanish live-life-to-the-fullest bravura and demonstrated how deep the experience of the cello could be in one quick hour.

Why not end this story by coming back to him?

Carlos recently told me he continues to teach and perform and has become an associate professor of cello in Vilagarcia de Arousa, a seaside town not far from the border with Portugal, in Pontevedra province.

Someday, we plan to play cellos together when I can arrange another visit to Spain. He still conducts lectures for National Geographic Adventures in Villafranca, where we first met him. If you ever find yourself on the Camino, I hope you're lucky enough to hear Carlos perform and talk. It will enhance your enjoyment of this fabulous instrument.

Though I've been learning to play for more than two years now, it still feels like I am just getting started, and I continue to be overwhelmed at the collective kindness of players and everyone associated with the cello.

It feels like an act of grace made this all happen. One description of grace is to receive unmerited divine favor. Grace is good fortune coming into your life unexpectedly. If that is the case, grace arranged for the cello to appear out of nowhere and prompted me to reinterpret how I understand the relationships with music I've had since I was a kid.

There are theories that spirituality is replacing formal, mainstream religion. Experts who study these trends say that we are becoming a secular people devoid of any connection with the divine. In reality, we can never become an entirely secular society lacking in spiritual growth so long as there are two cello players in the world available to perform a duet.

The intriguing connections and friendships that the cello facilitates appear when least expected. This week a new member of our extended family, Ken Bloom, texted in response to learning I played the cello: "CELLO!!!??? What are you playing? My favorite instrument (and the string instrument with the widest range). Our daughter played the cello for about 10 years."

If you're looking for something to have in common with someone you've just met, who you expect to be associated with for the foreseeable future, what better connection might you start with than sharing an inordinate regard for the cello.

My Camino continues long after reaching the great Santiago de Compostela Cathedral, as I keep learning to experience the cello in unexpected ways. These include: meeting new players, from experienced professional performers to beginners scratching out their first notes, luthiers making innovative instruments, attending live performances by string players, and assorted other explorations. I seek out chamber concerts where there's at least one cello in the ensemble and sit as close to them as possible to study the way they play. Weekly cello lessons continue too, which take me on circuitous routes leading to agreeably offbeat people.

I realize that I had not gone looking for the cello intentionally. Hadn't been seeking something, a great lesson or magnificent new challenge. The instrument found me on its own, is how I look at. The cello and its music and the people connected by devotion to the cello were reaching out all the time. There was no reason to go hunting to bring the cello into my life. Finding it just necessitated wandering into the right room, where the musician brought the instrument out and introduced it. It wasn't me who'd gone looking for something to latch onto.

It was The Cello Who Loved Me.

Acknowledgments

Many thanks to the Sorensen family, Susan, Kenzy, Bennett, and new addition, Phoebe Bloom. Editors and mentors: Katherine Flitsch, Lynn Hightower, Megan Rowe, Alexandra DuSablon, Shirin Leos, Kristin Thiel, Kate Peterson. Brett Hall-Jones and the mighty Community of Writers at Olympic Valley.

Bill Burleson and Mariann Bentz and the perky Flexible Press team. Support small, independent presses and bookstores, please. The greater universe of cello players, luthiers, bow makers, and everyone willing to generously fill me in on how they create, maintain, and play the most beautiful instrument in the world.

Creative powerhouse Mark Fearing and his help with cover concepts.

Fellow Camino and Scotland hikers Larry and Kathleen Paul.

Mary Ann Coggins Kaza, of course, fabled luthier Michael Doran, Ben Mason, Kelvin Scott, Diane Chaplin, Gretchen Yanover, Gideon Freudmann, Collin Oldham—more about him in another book, my inspiration Carlos Ariel Gracia Baez from Santiago de Compostela, charming Ruth Obermayer in Granada, Spain, Gjert Skjelbred, Marit Uhlving, and Doffen in Oslo and their mysterious secret island and yacht.

Julian Thompson and the Australian Chamber Orchestra in Sydney, Eric Trujillo and the Pachuco brothers in Colorado, Jacob von der Lippe telling the world the Strad is Dead from Oslo, Norway. Vik Vandamme in Belgium.

Crazy Jodi Norbey and the New Zealand Trails crew for your unbridled support. If you're headed to New Zealand, check out their tours and tell them George sent you.

The staff at David Kerr Violin Shop in Portland, Oregon. Portland Cello Project—please have a Christmas Concert every year.

The Smithsonian Museum of American History, the Smithsonian Chamber Society, and the remarkable Kenneth Slowik.

The UCLA Writing Program and Nutschell Windsor. Everyone who helped me share this story of the cello.

About the Author

George Sorensen worked as a marketing communications manager and tech writer for well over thirty years, contributing to companies and teams, including: the NASA Mars Program, 3M, where he was on the launch team for Post-it Notes and other products, Boeing drone aircraft, Nike cybersecurity, and sundry other entities. He is an Eagle Scout who created and wrote the pamphlet for the Composite Materials Merit Badge, educating youth in this STEM technology.

Additionally, George is the author of four published narrative nonfiction books, most recently the delightful *Hot Dish Confidential—That Year My Friends Taught Me to Cook* (Flexible Press, 2024), which has been compared to Peter Mayle's *A Year in Provence* and books by Bill Bryson. Walt Disney Studios optioned an unpublished novel back in the day, and he wishes they'd option another. In addition to narrative nonfiction, he also writes novels. George lives in Lake Oswego, Oregon, and travels the world with his Wisconsin-Norwegian wife, Susan.

He encourages you to start playing the cello.